THE EUCHARIST

A BIBLE STUDY GUIDE FOR CATHOLICS

FR. MITCH PACWA, S.J.

Our Sunday Visitor Publishing Division
Our Sunday Visitor, Inc.
Huntington, Indiana 46750

Nihil Obstat
Msgr. Michael Heintz, Ph.D.
Censor Librorum

Imprimatur
✠ Kevin C. Rhoades
Bishop of Fort Wayne-South Bend
November 19, 2012

The *Nihil Obstat* and *Imprimatur* are official declarations that a book is free from doctrinal or moral error. It is not implied that those who have granted the *Nihil Obstat* and *Imprimatur* agree with the contents, opinions, or statements expressed.

ISBN: 978-1-61278-670-4 (Inventory No. T1375)
eISBN: 978-1-61278-306-2
LCCN: 2012953420

Cover design: Lindsey Riesen
Cover art: The Crosiers
Interior design: Sherri L. Hoffman
Interior art: iStockPhoto.com

PRINTED IN THE UNITED STATES OF AMERICA

To Neil Fisher for his eightieth birthday,
to his wonderful wife, Gaelyn,
son Ben and his wife, Amy,
and son Matthew and his wife, Kerian,
in gratitude for the many years
they have invited me to their ranch to hunt.
These times of quiet and relaxation have been filled with
their warmth, friendship, and commitment to our Catholic faith.
I appreciate everything they have taught me
through introducing me to my favorite sport.

CONTENTS

HOW TO USE THIS STUDY GUIDE IN A GROUP

This is an interactive study guide. It can be read with profit either alone or as part of a group Bible study. Below are suggestions for the use of this book in a group.

WHAT YOU WILL NEED FOR EVERY SESSION

- This study guide
- A Bible
- A notebook

- **Before Session 1, members of the group are encouraged to read the Introduction and Session 1 and to complete all the exercises in both.** They should bring this study guide with them to the group session.
- **Begin the session with prayer** (for example, Prayer Before Study, on page 112).
- **Invite one person in the group to read one of the Scripture passages included in this session's material.**
- **Allow five minutes of silent reflection on the passage.** This allows the group to quiet their inner thoughts and to center themselves on the lesson to be discussed.
- **Catechesis:** Give all members a chance to share some point that they have learned about the Eucharist. Was this something new or a new insight into something? Was there anything that raised a question? (Allow fifteen to twenty minutes for this.)
- **Discussion:** Use the discussion questions at the end of the session chapter to begin a deeper grasp of the material covered in the session. (Allow fifteen to twenty minutes for this).

- **Conclusion:** Have all members of the group summarize the key concepts they learned about the Eucharist discussed in the session. Assign the next session as homework, to be completed before the next group session.

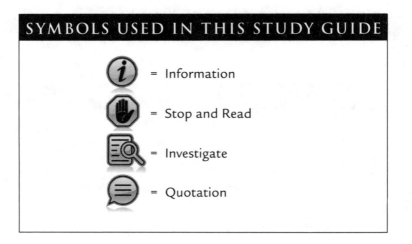

SYMBOLS USED IN THIS STUDY GUIDE

= Information

= Stop and Read

= Investigate

= Quotation

ACKNOWLEDGMENTS

Unless otherwise noted, the Scripture citations used in this work are taken from the Catholic Edition of the Revised Standard Version of the Bible (RSV), copyright © 1965, 1966 by the Division of Christian Education of the National Council of the Churches of Christ in the United States of America. Used by permission. All rights reserved.

Quotations from papal statements, Vatican II, and other Vatican documents are copyrighted, © 2013, Libreria Editrice Vaticana.

Excerpts from the English translation of The Roman Missal © 2010, International Commission on English in the Liturgy Corporation (ICEL). The English translation of the Gloria, the Nicene Creed, and the Agnus Dei is by the International Consultation on English Texts (ICET).

INTRODUCTION

> "The Eucharist makes constantly present the Risen Christ who continues to give himself to us, calling us to participate in the banquet of his Body and his Blood. From full communion with him flows every other element of the Church's life: first of all, communion among all the faithful, the commitment to proclaiming and witnessing to the Gospel, the ardor of love for all, especially the poorest and lowliest."
>
> — POPE BENEDICT XVI,
> First Message (April 20, 2005)

The Old Testament is very much part of Christian Scripture. In the Nicene Creed, we proclaim that the Holy Spirit "has spoken through the prophets," and we see that the New Testament quotes from the Old 360 times, in order to show how Jesus fulfills the prophecies. Jesus himself explained to the disciples on the way to Emmaus, "O foolish men, and slow of heart to believe all that the prophets have spoken! Was it not necessary that the Christ should suffer these things and enter into his glory?" (Lk 24:25-26). Later that night, he told the assembled disciples, as "he opened their minds to understand the scriptures": "Thus it is written, that the Christ should suffer and on the third day rise from the dead" (Lk 24:45-46). Therefore we do well to go to the Old Testament to better understand Christ's life in the context of the Judaism that he knew and lived.

CONSIDER

In this book, we want to examine Jesus' teaching and actions concerning the Eucharist, as found in the New Testament and as illumined by the Old Testament and Jewish practice. This will include a study of the connection between Old Testament sacrifices and the vocabulary that Jesus used from that context in the institution of the Eucharist (Session 2). Since he established the Eucharist at Passover, this, too, will be an obvious object of study (Session 5). This brings up the issue of the lamb of God, which John the Baptist identifies as Jesus (Jn 1:29), and which has its roots in Isaiah 53 and its fulfillment in Christ, as the New Testament, especially the Book of Revelation, explains (Session 3). The seriousness of Jesus' command to eat his flesh and drink his blood is explained in the context of Jesus demonstrating his divinity and summoning his disciples to complete faith in him (Session 4).

In the Old Testament, sacrifices were offered by the Levitical priests; in the New Testament, Jesus is the one, true, and eternal high priest according to the order of Melchizedek. We will look at the role of the Old Testament high priest in his primary function in the sacrifices on Yom Kippur, the Day of Atonement (Session 1) and at the role of Jesus, the eternal high priest of the new and eternal covenant (Session 6), as bookends for this study of the biblical roots of the Eucharist.

May this help us all to grow in faith and understanding of Christ's saving work in the Eucharist so that we can participate in it more richly and live it out in daily life. As Pope Benedict says, "I encourage all of you to discover ever more fully in the Eucharist, the sacrament of Christ's sacrificial love, the inspiration and strength needed to work ever more generously for the spread of God's Kingdom and the growth of the civilization of love (cf. *Sacramentum Caritatis*, n. 90)."

Session 1

OLD TESTAMENT BACKGROUND

"The priest who is anointed and ordained to succeed his father as high priest is to make atonement. He is to put on the sacred linen garments and make atonement for the Most Holy Place, for the tent of meeting and the altar, and for the priests and all the members of the community. This is to be a lasting ordinance for you. . . ."

— LEVITICUS 16:32-34

The Old Testament begins with eleven chapters on the origins of the human race and its development, with particular focus on the progenitors of the various nations. This story speaks of a fall from God's grace through human disobedience of God's commandment. Sin repeats itself at every stage of human development, with particular emphasis on the role of sin in the Flood and in the Tower of Babel. Two of these stories — Cain and Abel, and the end of the Flood — mention sacrifices as a normal part of worship, a theme that continues throughout the Old and New Testaments.

Genesis 12 changes perspective from general human history to the story of one elderly man from Mesopotamia — Abram. God took the initiative to call him to believe in the one God who created the world and promised to make him and his descendants a blessing for all the families of the world. Abram accepted this call, migrated to the land of Canaan, and upon arrival offered sacrifices at Shechem, Bethel, and Mamre, near Hebron. His descendants likewise built altars and offered sacrifices until they migrated to Egypt.

Stop here and read **Genesis 12:1-3**, **Genesis 12:6-8**, and **Genesis 13:18** in your own Bible.

Upon their liberation from slavery in Egypt, under Moses' prophetic leadership, a combination of moral commandments and liturgical legislation of worship, especially of sacrifices, was given by God through Moses on Mount Sinai. Worship of the only true God became the purpose of this people's existence, and many of the sacrifices, such as peace offerings, were oriented toward communion with the Lord God. However, as the biblical narratives of the people in Egypt and during the forty-year wandering in Sinai indicate, they, like all their human forebears, were sinners, including Moses and his brother Aaron the high priest.

OBEDIENCE TO GOD'S LAW

A central premise of Israel's religion was that moral integrity through obedience to God's Law was a necessary precondition for authentic worship of God. From God's demand for moral integrity flowed the ability of Israel to honestly admit the sins of the nation and even of its heroes — Noah's drunkenness, Abraham's lies about Sarah, Moses disobeying God at Meribah, David's adultery and murder of Uriah, Solomon's follies, etc. Such sins called for repentance by the sinners and the offering of sacrifices known as "sin offerings" and "guilt offerings." One particular day of the year was designated as Yom Kippur, the Day of Atonement, a day of prayer, strict fasting, and sacrifices for the sins of the nation.

The New Testament likewise assumes that human beings are sinners. Continuing the Old Testament genius, the New Testament writers tell episodes where the heroes of faith, such as the apostles, are shown to be sinners. In fact, the primary purpose of God becoming flesh in Jesus Christ was to offer himself as a sacrifice for the sins of the whole world by dying on a cross. His crucifixion is not portrayed merely as a tragedy of an innocent person dying unjustly but also as a sacrifice that takes away sin.

STUDY

One book of the New Testament, the Letter to the Hebrews, especially draws out the links between the Old Testament priesthood and sacrifices for sin, particularly on Yom Kippur, and Christ's fulfillment of the priesthood and sin offering.

Of course, we know that Jesus Christ instituted the Eucharist at the Last Supper during the Passover celebration in spring, and we will examine the connections with that feast later. At this point, however, we want to see the Eucharist in the broader context of the scriptural teaching of the Redemption, which includes the perspective of Hebrews' teaching on Jesus Christ the High Priest who offers himself as a sacrifice for the sins of the world. This will provide a basis for the sometimes neglected aspect of the Eucharist as a sacrifice, which Christ instituted for the new covenant he established.

Here we will examine the most important Israelite ceremonies and sacrifices for the forgiveness of sins at Yom Kippur, since Hebrews 9:1-14 connects Christ's priesthood and sacrifice to the celebration of Yom Kippur by the Jewish high priest. The Yom Kippur ceremonies contain some less well-known connections to Christ's saving action through his sacrifice on the cross, in preparation of our study of the Mass.

INVESTIGATE

ASPECTS OF SACRIFICE

 Look up the following passages and make notes on the various aspects of sacrifice:

PASSAGE	NOTES
Romans 8:3-4	
1 Corinthians 5:7	
1 Corinthians 15:3-4	
2 Corinthians 5:14-21	
Ephesians 5:2	
1 Peter 1:18-19	
Revelation 5:6, 12	

STUDY

Yom Kippur means the Day of Atonement, the holiest day of the Jewish calendar, dedicated to prayer and fasting. "Yom" means "day." "Kippur" is derived from a Hebrew verb meaning "to cover." When the blood of the sacrifices covers sins, God will no longer see the offenses and will accept the sacrifice that the priests offer him.

Only one Scripture passage describes the Day of Atonement: Leviticus 16:1-34. In addition, a number of details of this festival were preserved in Jewish traditions found outside the Bible. Since the Israelite priesthood was passed on from father to son, the fathers also passed on the traditions of the liturgy to their sons, in a way parallel to fathers passing on their trades and skills to their sons.

THE LEVITICAL PRIESTHOOD

Levitical priests had an obligation to raise a family because the priesthood belonged to the tribe of Levi only, and particularly to the clan Cohen, which is the Hebrew word for priest. Only boys born to a Cohen family could be eligible for the priesthood; men from the other eleven tribes were automatically excluded.

These Yom Kippur traditions were eventually written down by rabbis from the Pharisee party after the destruction of the Temple in A.D. 70. Many of the priests were killed in the sack of Jerusalem, but a leading rabbi, Johanan ben Zakkai, led his followers out of the city before it was destroyed. This community wrote down many traditions in a collection called the Mishna, which was finished around A.D. 200. Later rabbis added traditions to the Mishna in a much larger collection known as the Talmud. The Mishna tractate "Yoma" treats the celebration of Yom Kippur, and its liturgy, from which, along with Leviticus 16, we will try to understand the Yom Kippur rituals as a typology of Jesus Christ's sacrifice.

Yom Kippur starts on the tenth of the Jewish month Tishri, which begins at the autumn equinox in September. The high priest began to prepare for the feast on the third of Tishri by leaving his home to stay in the "Councillors' Chamber," a room inside the Temple's Nicanor Gate. Another priest was also prepared, in case the high priest became ineligible to offer the sacrifices through ritual uncleanness or an accident. In fact, another wife was made ready for him, in case his own wife died, so that he would have a family and be able to "make atonement for himself and his house" (Lev 16:6). During this week, he was required to participate in the daily sacrifices (Ex 29:38ff), burn the incense (Ex 30:1-8), and trim the lamps (Ex 27:20-21), all of which was optional for him to perform personally on other days of the year (see Yoma 1:1-2).

CONSIDER

Two points can be made about Christ in relationship to this section of Yoma. First, Jesus Christ does not need an alternate priest because, as God the Son, he is eternal and will hold his priesthood forever. The provision for preparation of a second candidate for high priest in case something untoward happened to the appointed high priest highlights a point made in Hebrews 7:23-24: "The former priests were many in number, because they were prevented by death from continuing in office; but he [Jesus] holds his priesthood permanently, because he continues forever." This is not a priesthood inherited from an earthly father, as was the Levitical priesthood, but an eternal priesthood bestowed by God's oath. Therefore Christ does not need an alternate to take his place in case he dies. In fact, his death on the cross will not obviate his priesthood but will be its primary action.

Second, there is a parallel between Jesus and the high priest entering the Temple a week before Yom Kippur. Jesus entered Jerusalem on Palm Sunday and stayed throughout the whole week teaching in the Temple. He could not live inside it, since he was not a Levitical priest, but he spent his last week teaching inside the Temple.

We can develop this connection a bit further. While the priest stayed within the Temple, the elders would read to him the liturgy of Yom Kippur daily and require him to memorize Leviticus 16 and the other traditions of the liturgy. On the morning before Yom Kippur, they would bring oxen, rams, and sheep so that he would know exactly how to perform the sacrifices (Yoma 1:3). The elders then made the priest swear by God, who dwells in the Temple, that he would change nothing they had taught him (Yoma 1:5).

The priest needed this time of preparation and spent more time in prayer too, reading Job, Chronicles, Ezra, and Daniel — books written after the Babylonian exile (Yoma 1:6).

THE DANGERS OF LITURGICAL ABUSE

Celebrating the liturgy incorrectly was dangerous, as when Nadab and Abihu were struck dead for liturgical abuse (Lev 10:1-3). Later, the high priest Eli warned his sons, Hophni and Phineas, about their immorality and liturgical abuses (1 Sam 2:22-25), and an anonymous prophet condemned them for their liturgical abuse (1 Sam 2:27-36). The Philistines then captured the Ark of the Covenant and killed Hophni and Phineas, as had been prophesied (1 Sam 4:11, 17).

When Jesus Christ entered Jerusalem on Palm Sunday to prepare for his high priestly ministry of dying on the cross and then rising from the dead, he first went to the Temple and cleansed it of moneychangers and sellers of animals (Mt 21:12-13; Mk 11:15-16). Then he remained there, not listening to the Scriptures and ritual instructions, but in fulfilling them and in making new Scriptures. In fact, his entrance into Jerusalem on an ass fulfills Zechariah 9:9-10 (see Mt 21:1-8; Mk 11:1-8; Lk 19:29-38). Daily he taught the people in the Temple and disputed with the Pharisees and Sadducees on a variety of topics, and that teaching has become a significant section of the Gospels.

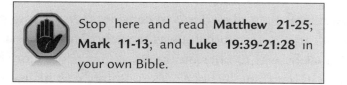

Stop here and read **Matthew 21-25**; **Mark 11-13**; and **Luke 19:39-21:28** in your own Bible.

The fact that the high priest of the new covenant, Jesus Christ, teaches the elders, sages, and priests during the week of preparation for his great sacrificial act indicates his superior priesthood in yet another way.

CONSIDER

Christians may reflect on two ways this week of how preparation affects their own practice. First, Holy Week is still a time for the whole Church to read the Scriptures, reflect, pray, and fast in anticipation of the Triduum, when we celebrate the great event of Christ's redeeming death and resurrection.

Second, just as the high priest had to swear an oath not to change a single component of the Yom Kippur liturgy, similarly, a Catholic priest may not change the liturgy, since it is not his Mass. The Mass belongs primarily to Jesus Christ and secondly to the Church, so it is not the priest's to change, as Vatican II said: "Therefore no other person, not even a priest, may add, remove, or change anything in the liturgy on his own authority" (*Sacrosanctum Concilium*, n. 22.3).

Yet one other interesting connection to the high priest's oath to change nothing in the liturgy comes in Gethsemane. Consider our Lord's prayer in Gethsemane, that the Father remove the cup of suffering from him.

> Stop here and read **Matthew 26:39**; **Mark 14:35-36**; and **Luke 22:41-42**; see also **Hebrews 5:7** in your own Bible.

However, as painful as it was to consider the suffering to come, Jesus also came to accept that it was the very core of the sacrifice of himself that he was to offer on the cross. Therefore Christ added, "not my will but thine be done." Jesus' liturgy was his passion and death, and on the night before he suffered he explicitly made the commitment to see it through — a far more heroic commitment than a resolution to celebrate the rubrics of the liturgy correctly.

Still another parallel to Gethsemane is found in the Yom Kippur practice of having the younger priests stay up all night with the high priest to prevent him from falling asleep before the feast began. They diverted him until the "time of slaughtering drew near" (Yoma 1:7), lest he have a nocturnal pollution and disqualify himself from offering the sacrifices. Jesus, the high priest according to the order of Melchizedek, asked his disciples — his priests newly ordained at the Last Supper — to stay up with him in Gethsemane and watch. However, they were the ones who kept falling asleep, and he, the High Priest, had to wake them up before the betrayal and Passion began.

STUDY

The Yom Kippur ceremonies began when the first light of day entered the tomb of Abraham in the city of Hebron, south of Jerusalem, to indicate that dawn had truly commenced (Yoma 3:1-2a). A system of signals indicated when this occurred in Hebron so that the priests knew when to start in Jerusalem. Hebron was the touchstone of dawn because in Genesis 22:3 Abraham set out from there at dawn to sacrifice his son Isaac on Mount Moriah, which was the Temple Mount in Jerusalem. Abraham, therefore, made the first morning sacrifice mentioned in the Bible, at which the Lord tested him with the command to sacrifice his son, and he obeyed. On the way up Mount Moriah (Gen 22:7-8), Isaac asked: "Behold, the fire and the wood [which Isaac was carrying]; but where is the lamb for a burnt offering?" Abraham answered, "God will provide," and proceeded to sacrifice Isaac until the angel of the Lord stopped him. Abraham's willingness to sacrifice Isaac connects with the Gospel, where God provided the Lamb of sacrifice, his own Son, Jesus Christ, who carried the wood of his cross up Mount Calvary. While God's angel stopped Abraham's sacrifice of his son, God let his own Son die as the sacrificial Lamb who takes away the sins of the world (see Jn 1:29).

After trumpet blasts announced the Day of Atonement, the high priest removed his clothes and took the first of five baths by immersion, a step necessary for entrance into the inner court of the Temple. He put on gold vestments and offered the daily morning sacrifice of a lamb, which was burned and offered with bread and wine (Yoma 3:2b-4). Twelve priests accompanied him as he offered the morning lamb, which parallels Jesus making twelve apostles into priests at the Last Supper.

BAPTISM BY BLOOD

Just before Christ came to Jerusalem, James and John asked to be seated at his right and left. He asked them, "Are you able to drink the cup that I drink, or to be baptized with the baptism with which I am baptized?" (Mk 10:38). Christ was clearly referring to his suffering in general. Yet the scourging at the pillar became a type of bath in blood as the whip tore his flesh to the bone, which makes the "baptism" more specific. The term "baptism" may allude to the high priest's immersions before offering his sacrifices, which are called "ablutions" (in the Greek text, the word is "baptisms") in Hebrews 9:10, as a further link to these ideas. Still later, the Christian Sacrament of Baptism will become a prerequisite for participating in the Eucharistic sacrifice.

Next, the priest stripped off his vestments, immersed himself in a second bath, and put on white vestments and washed his hands (Lev 16:4; Yoma 3:6). He then approached a bull standing between the porch and the altar, with its head south but its face turned west, to the Holy of Holies — and Calvary. The high priest placed his hands between the horns, with his thumbs crossed over, and confessed his sins, to place them on the bull: "O God, I have committed iniquity, transgressed and sinned before Thee, I and my house. . . . [F]or on this day shall atonement be made for you, to cleanse you; from all your sins you shall be clean before the LORD." This was the first time the high priest pronounced the divine Name, so the people responded: "Blessed be the name of the glory of his kingdom forever" (Yoma 3:8; Lev 16:3-4, 30).

THE NAME OF THE LORD

The Second Commandment says, "Thou shalt not take the Name of the Lord thy God in vain." A key principle of Pharisaic Judaism was called "putting a fence around Torah," meaning that other regulations would be added in order to prevent Jews from

continued on next page…

breaking the commandments. To prevent Jews from taking the divine Name in vain, even inadvertently, a law was made prohibiting Jews from ever pronouncing it. When they see it written in the Bible, they pronounce the word "Lord" instead, and on other occasions they simply refer to "the Name." Only the high priest could speak the Name out loud, and then only once a year during the Yom Kippur celebrations.

The Letter to the Hebrews highlights the high priest's need to bring sacrifices for his own sins and then those of the people: "into the second [Holy of Holies] only the high priest goes, and he but once a year, and not without taking blood which he offers for himself and for the errors of the people" (Heb 9:7). In contrast, Jesus did not have to make a sin offering because he was without sin, either original sin or any actual sin. Instead, he offered himself for the sins of the rest of the world.

As it says in Hebrews 9:11-14:

> But when Christ appeared as a high priest of the good things that have come, then through the greater and more perfect tent (not made with hands, that is, not of this creation) he entered once for all into the Holy Place, taking not the blood of goats and calves but his own blood, thus securing an eternal redemption. For if the sprinkling of defiled persons with the blood of goats and bulls and with the ashes of a heifer sanctifies for the purification of the flesh, how much more shall the blood of Christ, who through the eternal Spirit offered himself without blemish to God, purify your conscience from dead works to serve the living God.

STUDY

Next, the high priest and two other priests would go to the north of the altar, where there were two he-goats of equal appearance, size, and value, bought at the same time (Yoma 6:1), and a box containing two pieces of paper with the words "For Azazel" and "For the Lord" (Yoma 3:9). (Azazel was a demon who dwelled in the desert.) The high priest shook the box and chose a lot with each hand, and he would raise whichever hand held the lot that read, "For the Lord," and then placed the lots on the head of each goat, pronouncing out loud, "For the Lord," the second time the divine Name was spoken. The priest tied a crimson thread on the head of the goat "For Azazel," which was the scapegoat, and a thread around the neck of the goat "For the Lord." The priest then placed his hands on the heads of the goats (Leviticus 16:5, 7-8; Yoma 4:1-2).

Incidentally, the Talmud on Yoma mentions that the right hand was not on the goat for the Lord for the forty years before the destruction of the Temple. This means that from the time of Christ's death and resurrection, the right hand was no longer on the head of the goat for the Lord. We might see a parallel to this ceremony at Jesus' trial before Pilate, when he offers the people a choice between Barabbas the murderer and Jesus. The high priests instigated the people to choose Barabbas over Jesus, letting the murderer go free. Jesus, the only begotten Son of God, parallels the goat "For the Lord," while Barabbas, whose name in Aramaic means "son of the father," becomes the goat who escapes.

The high priest then returned to his bullock, laid two hands on it, and confessed his sins and repeated Leviticus 16:30, pronouncing the divine Name a third time (Lev 16:6; Yoma 4:20). Then he slaughtered the bull and put its blood in a basin, which another priest kept stirring to prevent coagulation (Lev 16:11; Yoma 4:3). Next he took hot coals from the altar and placed them in a censer (Yoma 4:4) and put two handfuls of the very finest incense in a ladle and brought it all inside the curtains separating the Holy Place from the Holy of Holies (Lev 16:11; Yoma 5:1). He placed the censer on a rock inside the Holy of Holies known as the Shetiyah ("Foundation") that remained there after the Ark had been removed in previous centuries. The smoke of the incense filled the room so that he would not see the Ark of the Covenant (which was actually absent) and die (Lev 16:12-13; Yoma 5:2). (The other priests tied a rope around the high priest's leg so that if he died in the Holy of Holies, they could drag his corpse out without going into the Holy of Holies and end up dying themselves.)

STUDY

The high priest went back outside to get the basin containing the bull's blood and returned to the Holy of Holies to sprinkle it on the place where the Ark had been — once downward and seven times upward, "as though he were wielding a whip." He placed the basin with the remaining blood on a golden stand in the Holy Place (Lev 16:14; Yoma 5:3).

While in the Holy Place, he killed the he-goat, put its blood in a basin, and entered the Holy of Holies a third time to sprinkle the goat's blood once upward and seven times downward on the place where the Ark had been. He exchanged the basin of goat's blood for the basin of bull's blood and sprinkled the outside of the curtain of the Holy of Holies, and he then did the same with the goat's blood. Next he mixed the blood of the bull and the goat together (Lev 16:15-17; Yoma 5:4), and this mixture was sprinkled on the golden altar of incense before the Lord and the inner altar (Yoma 5:5). The blood remaining in the basin was poured at the base of the altar, and it flowed through a channel into the Kedron Valley east of the Temple, where it was sold as fertilizer.

Hebrews refers to the sprinkling with the blood of the bull and goat in the perspective of Jesus Christ. In the ninth chapter of Hebrews, the sprinkling with the blood of animals purifies externally, in accord with the old covenant at Sinai, with the passage beginning

> For if the sprinkling of defiled persons with the blood of goats and bulls and with the ashes of a heifer sanctifies for the purification of the flesh, . . . (Heb 9:13)

However, the blood of Christ purifies one's conscience interiorly as the result of the new covenant that promises an inheritance of eternal life, with the passage ending

> . . . how much more shall the blood of Christ, who through the eternal Spirit offered himself without blemish to God, purify your conscience from dead works to serve the living God. Therefore he is the mediator of a new covenant, so that those

who are called may receive the promised eternal inheritance, since a death has occurred which redeems them from the transgressions under the first covenant. (Heb 9:14-15)

The power of Christ's blood to cleanse consciences of sin derives from the fact that he is infinite God and a human who is capable of shedding blood.

Another passage in Hebrews makes a stronger reference to the "year after year" sacrifices on Yom Kippur:

For since the law has but a shadow of the good things to come instead of the true form of these realities, it can never, by the same sacrifices which are continually offered year after year, make perfect those who draw near. Otherwise, would they not have ceased to be offered? If the worshipers had once been cleansed, they would no longer have any consciousness of sin. But in these sacrifices there is a reminder of sin year after year. (Heb 10:1-3)

TIME FRAME

Note that Hebrews 10:2 indicates that the Yom Kippur sacrifices had not yet ceased to take place, thereby placing the writing of Hebrews to a time before the Jewish Revolt (A.D. 66) or the destruction of the Temple (A.D. 70).

Jesus, who always did the Father's will and accepted his will in Gethsemane, even to the death on the cross, fulfills the words of Psalm 40:8. Therefore Christ's accomplishing of the Father's will effects a new covenant in his own blood, as he states at the Last Supper, and the Christian believer becomes sanctified through the offering of Jesus' body "once and for all."

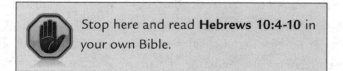

Stop here and read **Hebrews 10:4-10** in your own Bible.

After the return from the Babylonian Exile, the Holy of Holies no longer contained the Ark of the Covenant. The priest was supposed to sprinkle the blood on the mercy seat, but the place was empty. We Christians do not sprinkle a place with the blood of Christ, but we receive it interiorly. We each are a temple of the Holy Spirit, and we are the place where the blood is received, and the whole Church is now the temple. Incidentally, the veil of the Temple was made of wool of different colors. It required three hundred men to move it. In Yoma 9, the text mentions that forty years before the Temple was destroyed, the door of the Temple opened by itself. When Jesus died, the curtain of the Temple split from the top down, in the very year that Yoma indicates the door opened by itself. By tearing from the top down, it indicates that the tearing was an act of God and not of man, which would have been from the bottom up. Christ's death not only fulfills the Old Testament but also brings some elements of Yom Kippur to an end.

STUDY

After the ceremony of the sprinkling of the blood was finished, the high priest went to the scapegoat, laid both hands on it, and confessed the sins of the nation of Israel and repeated Leviticus 16:30, pronouncing the divine Name a fourth time, and the people again praised the Name (Lev 16:20-21; Yoma 6:2).

The scapegoat was an actual goat that was driven into the desert as part of the ceremonies of the Day of Atonement.

At that point, they gave the goat to a Gentile to lead it out of the city, though any Israelite could have done this (Yoma 6:3). As the goat was led out, people pulled at the goat's hair and shouted, "Bear [our sins] and be gone." The Gentile took the goat over the Mount of Olives to a cliff about twelve miles away (Lev 16:22; Yoma 6:4). Upon arrival, he divided the crimson woolen thread in half and tied half between the goat's horns and half on a rock. Then he pushed the goat over the cliff, where it rolled down the ravine and died. He walked back to a booth set up along the way and waited there until sundown.

We might see some connections between the scapegoat and Christ. Like the scapegoat, Jesus was led out of Jerusalem by Gentile Roman guards and a centurion, and this is a symbol of Christ dying for our sins outside the city:

> For the bodies of those animals whose blood is brought into the sanctuary by the high priest as a sacrifice for sin are burned outside the camp. So Jesus also suffered outside the gate in order to sanctify the people through his own blood. Therefore let us go forth to him outside the camp and bear the abuse he endured. (Heb 13:11-13)

However, while the scapegoat is innocent of sin, as are all animals, it is a very limited creature and has no inherent power to actually bear the sins of human beings who offend the infinite God. Christ, who was crucified on Calvary, which was just outside a western gate of Jerusalem, pays the debt of sin in full by his death. Christ is God made flesh, "For in him the whole fullness of deity dwells bodily" (Col 2:9), and therefore his death, completely unlike the scapegoat's, has infinite value. On that basis, St. Paul can say that Christ has "canceled the bond which stood against us with its legal demands; this he set aside, nailing it to the cross" (Col 2:14). Though the sins of each of us have an infinite value, since they offend the infinite and all-good God, Christ's death has infinite value that far exceeds our sins. While no goat can make up for human sin, no sin is more powerful than the death of the Son of God on the cross of Calvary.

On Yom Kippur, while the scapegoat was led to its death for the people's sins, the high priest in the Temple returned to the bull and the goat he had sacrificed so that he could cut them open and prepare the sacrificial portions to be burned on the altar. The offal was carried inside the skin to a place outside the city for burning (Lev 16:23-25; Yoma 6:7).

With the help of a series of signal towels that were waved along the scapegoat's route, the high priest would know that the scapegoat had died. At that report, and as the bull and the goat were being burned in sacrifice, the high priest would read Leviticus 16 and 23:26-32 and recite Numbers 29:7-11 from memory to the people as a testimony that the ceremonies had been faithfully carried out. He also pronounced eight benedictions for the Law, the Temple Service, the Thanksgiving, the Forgiveness of sins, the Temple, the Israelites, the priests, and a general prayer (Yoma 7:1).

SCARLET WOOL

Rabbi Ishmael said that a thread of crimson wool that had been tied to the Sanctuary door would at that point turn white in fulfillment of Isaiah 1:18: "Though your sins are like scarlet, they shall be as white as snow; though they are red like crimson, they shall become like wool." In the Talmud (Yoma 9:58-59), it was said that the wool stopped turning white for the forty years before the destruction of the Temple — that is, since the time of Christ's redemption on the cross.

The high priest then stripped off his clothes, immersed himself again, and put on his gold vestments and washed his hands and feet. Then he offered a ram for himself, one for the people, and seven unblemished year-old lambs, in accord with Numbers 29:7-11, for the celebration of Yom Kippur (Yoma 7:3).

He again washed his hands and feet, stripped from the gold vestments, and immersed himself in water, put on white vestments, and washed his hands and feet again — all so that he could bring out a ladle of incense and a censer. He washed his hands and feet, stripped, immersed himself, put on the golden vestments, and offered the daily afternoon lamb at three o'clock. Then he washed his hands and feet, stripped, and put on his own clothing. At this point, he went home and made a feast with his friends because he had "come forth safely from the Sanctuary" (Yoma 7:4). Remember, any liturgical abuse would have resulted in his death, so the successful celebration of the ceremonies meant he could live.

Perhaps we can see this feast celebrating the high priest's survival as a sign of the Resurrection, since Jesus rose from the dead after becoming a sacrifice, in which he truly did die. Then he gathered with his disciples and ate with them on the night of his resurrection:

> When he was at table with them, he took the bread and blessed, and broke it, and gave it to them. And their eyes were opened and they recognized him; and he vanished out of their sight. (Lk 24:30-31)

> And while they still disbelieved for joy, and wondered, he said to them, "Have you anything here to eat?" They gave him a piece of broiled fish, and he took it and ate before them. (Lk 24:41-43)

CONSIDER

The details of the Yom Kippur ceremonies are mostly unknown to Christians, and as a result the references to them in the Letter to the Hebrews make that book seem very obscure. Not only might an understanding of the feast illuminate the references in Hebrews, but also it helps us see the important connection between sacrifice and the forgiveness of sins in both the Old and New Testaments. This also sets the stage for seeing the significance of the sacrificial aspect of the Mass.

DISCUSS

1. What are some of the things you learned about the Yom Kippur ceremonies that might have been new or surprising?

2. What connections between Jesus' death and the sacrifices of the Day of Atonement that are discussed in Hebrews now are more relevant to your understanding of Jesus' sacrifice for us?
3. What new insights into the Eucharist have you gained from the Scripture passages in this chapter?

PRACTICE

This week, consider the implication of Jesus' becoming the "scape-goat" for your sins. Make an Act of Contrition or receive the Sacrament of Reconciliation, believing that through the Cross and Resurrection, you are now freed from the curse of sin.

Session 2

WORDS OF SACRIFICE

> "For the liturgy, 'through which the work of our redemption is accomplished,' most of all in the divine sacrifice of the Eucharist, is the outstanding means whereby the faithful may express in their lives, and manifest to others, the mystery of Christ and the real nature of the true Church."
>
> — *Sacrosanctum Concilium* (n. 2)

Since the very beginning, the Church has taught two points about the Eucharist: it is the Real Presence of the Body and Blood of Jesus Christ, and it is the re-presentation of Christ's sacrifice on the cross. Since the 1960s, some Catholics have either denied or, more likely, neglected both of these doctrines of the Real Presence and the sacrificial nature of the Mass. The ignorance has become so widespread that one time, in a conversation with a very well-educated seminarian, I surprised him by pointing out that each of the four primary Eucharistic Prayers of the Roman Rite explicitly mention the word "sacrifice" in the prayers. He doubted me, though he had been attending daily Mass for years, until he reread each prayer privately and then confirmed that this was true.

Sacrosanctum Concilium, the Second Vatican Council's Constitution on the Sacred Liturgy, says that "especially in the divine sacrifice of the Eucharist, 'the work of our redemption is accomplished' " (n. 2). The document declares further that "the liturgy is the summit toward which the activity of the Church is directed" and that the baptized "take part in the Sacrifice and . . . eat the Lord's Supper" (n. 10). Since the Second Vatican Council emphasized the sacrificial

THE REAL PRESENCE AND PROTESTANT THOUGHT

 In a two-volume study of the history of the doctrine of the Eucharist, a Protestant scholar, Darwell Stone, discovered that every theologian of the first thousand years of the Church taught the Catholic doctrines about the Eucharist. In the eleventh century, a French theologian, Berengarius, denied the Real Presence of Christ in the Eucharist, but after the idea of transubstantiation was explained to him, it made sense, and he returned to the Catholic faith. His denial of the Real Presence was revived in later centuries by John Wycliff and Jan Hus, and through their influence, by various Protestant Reformers. Additionally, some of these Reformers denied the sacrificial nature of the Mass.

element so strongly, we do well to understand that aspect better. Further, the council summoned the Church to search the Scriptures to understand the faith. Therefore, we will examine the scriptural roots of understanding the sacrificial elements of the Mass, beginning with the words used in the institution of the Eucharist at the Last Supper, in light of relevant terms in both the Old and New Testaments.

THEOLOGY AND THE WORD OF GOD

 Sacred theology rests on the written word of God, together with sacred Tradition, as its primary and perpetual foundation. By scrutinizing in the light of faith all truth stored up in the mystery of Christ, theology is most powerfully strengthened and constantly rejuvenated by that word. For Sacred Scriptures contain the word of God; and since they are inspired, they really are the word of God. And so, the study of the sacred page is, as it were, the soul of sacred theology (*Dei Verbum*, n. 24).

CONSIDER

Three Gospels and one of St. Paul's epistles include narratives of the institution of the Eucharist. John's Gospel has a long and extremely important teaching on the meaning of the Eucharist, which we will examine later, but no description of the institution. Of the four Institution Narratives we possess, the earliest is probably 1 Corinthians 11:23-26, written about A.D. 54; the Gospels probably come a bit later. The strongest similarities are seen between Paul and Luke, who was his traveling companion, and between Matthew and Mark. All four have basic similarities, but these two pairs contain specific wordings distinctive of each pair. All of them are important, and we will study each aspect of these texts. Therefore, all four texts are placed here as we study the sacrificial components of the words and phrases in their Old Testament background.

INVESTIGATE

THE INSTITUTION OF THE EUCHARIST

 Read the following narratives. Write down what each writer says about the institution of the Eucharist at the Last Supper, along with any insights you might have:

PASSAGE	NOTES
Matthew 26:26-28	
Mark 14:22-24	
Luke 22:19-20	
1 Corinthians 11:23-26	

STUDY

The first clue to the sacrificial nature of the Mass comes from the use of a present passive participle Christ uses to explain that in the new covenant, his blood "is being shed, poured out" (*evkunnomenon*). This verb appears in the Greek translation of the Old Testament (known as the Septuagint, LXX) 137 times, with a number of interesting meanings. Numerous times it refers to killing people and pouring out their blood.

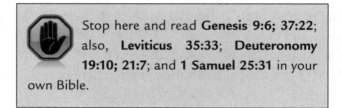

Stop here and read **Genesis 9:6; 37:22**; also, **Leviticus 35:33; Deuteronomy 19:10; 21:7**; and **1 Samuel 25:31** in your own Bible.

In Exodus 4:9, the text refers to Moses pouring out the water turned into blood. It frequently refers to pouring out the blood of animals, particularly in sacrifices.

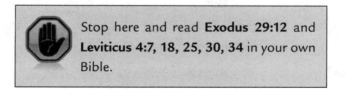

Stop here and read **Exodus 29:12** and **Leviticus 4:7, 18, 25, 30, 34** in your own Bible.

Though the word has other meanings, such as to pour out one's soul before the Lord, the meaning that best fits our Lord's use at the consecration of his precious Blood derives from the frequent uses of the word in sacrifices.

This raises some key differences between the Old Testament and the New Testament sacrifices. The animals of the Old Testament sacrifices did not have a free will, so they could not agree to being sacrificed. In the New Testament, Jesus freely chooses to offer his blood for the many who are sinners. The sacrificial animals did not share the same nature as those for whom the sacrifice was offered, while

Jesus did share the same human nature of the sinners for whom he died. Furthermore, Jesus also had a divine nature, so that his infinite greatness could be an adequate offering for offenses against the divine majesty. As Venerable Archbishop Fulton Sheen pointed out many times, an offense acquires its seriousness from the one who has been offended. Therefore, though it is serious to hurt one's neighbor, it is still more serious to hurt the president or the pope because of their offices. If we offend God, the offense is infinite, and it requires an infinite sacrifice to pay that infinite debt. For that reason, God himself had to become the sacrifice for sins against the divine majesty. Jesus Christ fulfills this perfectly.

A second way in which the words of the institution indicate their sacrificial nature is in the phrase describing Jesus' blood as that of a "new covenant" in 1 Corinthians 11:25 and Luke 22:20. The Old Testament background lies in Exodus 24:8, after Moses had placed half of the blood of twelve young bulls in bowls and had splashed the other half on the altar (Ex 24:5-6). He read the book of the covenant to the assembled Israelites, who agreed to obey and do all that the Lord had said: "Then Moses took and sprinkled the blood on the people and said, 'Behold, the blood of the covenant which Yahweh has made with you concerning all these words' " (Ex 24:8, author's translation).

This was the sealing of the old covenant with the blood of sacrifice, and likewise must the new covenant be sealed with the blood of Jesus' sacrifice. Instead of an external sprinkling with the blood of bulls, as in the old covenant, Jesus gives us his own blood and commands that his disciples drink it, taking it interiorly. He explains the importance of drinking his blood in John 6:53-56:

> Amen, amen, I say to you, unless you eat the flesh of the Son of man and drink his blood you do not have life within you. The one who eats my flesh and drinks my blood has life eternal, and I will raise him up on the last day. For my flesh is true food and my blood is true drink. The one who eats my flesh and drinks my blood remains in me and I in him. (Author's translation)

Jesus makes the eating of his flesh and the drinking of his blood of the new covenant a requirement for remaining with him in this life and in eternal life. He becomes the very nourishment of our souls.

A third element from the words of institution points to the sacrificial nature of the Mass — namely, our Lord's command for the apostles to "do" this (Lk 24:19; 1 Cor 11:24, 25). In most languages, the word "do, make" has a wide range of meanings; one of its frequent uses in the Old Testament means to offer sacrifice, as appears in many texts.

"WE MAY DO"

 The earliest such usage of the word "do" to mean "offer sacrifice" appears in the last conversation between Moses and Pharaoh, after the plague of darkness. Pharaoh agreed to allow the Israelites to go worship in the desert. In Exodus 10:25, Moses said: "You must also let us have sacrifices and burnt offerings, that we may sacrifice to the LORD our God." The word translated as "sacrifice" here is actually *asinu*, "we may do." The Septuagint similarly uses *poiesomen*, "we do," in its translation. Both the Hebrew text and the Septuagint version of this verse use the verb "do." The Latin Vulgate translates this verb as *offeramus*, and the Revised Standard Version and King James translate it by the word "sacrifice." This is certainly correct and communicates the sense of the term here and elsewhere in the Old Testament.

STUDY

Many other occurrences of using the word "do" to mean "sacrifice" occur in Leviticus and Numbers, when the texts treat the regulation of different kinds of sacrifices. A very interesting context for the use of "do" with the meaning of sacrifice is the ordination of Aaron and his sons as priests in Leviticus 8-9, since the Church has regarded Christ's command to the apostles to "do this" as their ordination to his priesthood of the new covenant.

In Leviticus 8:1-4, the ordination begins with assembling Aaron, his sons, a bull of the sin offering, two rams, unleavened bread, the anointing oil, and the people. Then the candidates for priesthood are washed and clothed in sacred vestments (Lev 8:5-9) and the tabernacle and Aaron are anointed with oil, and Aaron's sons are vested (Lev 8:10-13). The next series of actions are the sacrifices.

First is the bull of the sin offering, which, after Aaron and his sons lay hands on it, while they confess their sins, Moses "slaughters" (*wayishhat*) and burns it (Lev 8:14-17). They repeat this with the first ram (Lev 8:18-21), while the second ram is the ordination ram, whose blood is daubed on the priests' rights ears, thumbs, and big toes (Lev 8:22-25). The animal fat along with an unleavened loaf, an oil cake, and a wafer are waved by the new priests, before Moses burns them as a sweet-smelling sacrifice (Lev 8:26-29). Moses then sprinkles the new priests with oil and blood (Lev 8:30) and orders them to boil meat and eat it, and to remain in the Tent of Meeting for a seven-day ordination period (Lev 8:31-36). A relevant verse for our word use is Leviticus 8:34, "the LORD has commanded to do to make atonement for you" (author's translation). The atonement is an action that they "do" as a general description of the seven days of ordination atonement sacrifices.

On the eighth day, Moses requires the priests to "bring near before the LORD" a bull for a sin offering and a ram for a burnt offering (Lev 9:1-2), and he commands the people to bring a male goat for a sin offering, a calf and a lamb for a burnt offering, an ox and a ram for peace offerings, and a cereal offering mixed with oil in preparation for the Lord's appearance to them (Lev 9:3-6). He uses the word "do" in his command to offer these sacrifices (Lev 9:7): "Draw near to the altar, and offer your sin offering and your burnt offering, and make atonement for yourself and for the people; and bring the offering of the people, and make atonement for them; as the LORD has commanded." The phrase "offer your sin offering" is "do the sin offering," and "bring the offering of the people" is literally "do the offering (*qorban*) of the people and atone for them." This order to "do" offerings is commanded by the Lord, much as Jesus commands the apostles at the Last Supper to "do this" in his memory.

There are more texts which use the Hebrew word "do" to mean "sacrifice," and the Greek Septuagint usually keeps the word "do," though, as noted above, it may translate "do" with the Greek word for "sacrifice." This indicates that not only in the original Hebrew but also in the Jewish translation of the Bible into Greek, "do" can refer to "sacrifice."

Certainly "do" also has a number of other meanings, and context is the best determinant for knowing which meaning best fits a passage, as has been true of all the passages treated in this section. Therefore, further study of the context of the Last Supper terminology is necessary to determine whether "do this in my memory" has a sacrificial sense.

"TO DO" AND CLEANSING LEPROSY

 Another use of "do" meaning sacrifice is Leviticus 14, which treats various laws for offering sacrifice and cleansing leprosy in persons and things. However, it is worth noting that this passage uses the English word "offer" four times to translate three different Hebrew words. "Offer" in Leviticus 14:12 translates the Hebrew word "bring near" or "cause to come near." "Offer" in Leviticus 14:19 translates the Hebrew word "do": "The priest shall offer [do] the sin offering, to make atonement for him who is to be cleansed from his uncleanness. And afterward he shall kill the burnt offering." Again "offer" translates "do" in Leviticus 14:30-31. In the law of cleansing and offering sacrifice for the leper, the Hebrew word "do" is used two out of four times to translate the verbal concept of offering.

CONSIDER

The fourth point of the Institution Narrative suggesting sacrifice is doing it as a memorial of Jesus. Some want to understand the memorial as a merely human calling to mind of the last Passover meal our Lord celebrated. This neither grasps the Old Testament understanding of memory nor the importance of memorial terminology in association with sacrifices.

Modern commentators accept that remembering included some sense of making present the object of the memory. For instance, Amos 6:10 warns, "Hush, do not remember Yahweh by name," and Psalm 20:8 (Ps 20:7 in English) proclaims, "But we in the name of Yahweh our God will cause remembrance" (author's translation). This understanding of memory as making present points to the Real Presence of the Lord Jesus in the sacrament he instituted at the Last Supper.

INVESTIGATE

The sacrificial sense of remembering appears in the Old Testament use of memorial terminology for sacrifices. All occurrences of "memorial" refer to the sweet-smelling smoke of incense offered with a sacrifice of meal and oil.

Look up the following verses and note what they say about memorials and sacrifice:

- Leviticus 2:1
- Leviticus 2:16
- Leviticus 5:12
- Leviticus 24:7
- Numbers 5:26
- Exodus 17:14

This list of verses brings out that various objects were used simply to help remember past events and teachings or liturgies. However, these are not the only uses of the term "memorial" (*zikaron*). Another use is very relevant to the use of "memorial" in Jesus' words at the institution of the Eucharist. It also refers to certain sacrifices, especially meal offerings. Look up the following two verses and note how they explicitly link the word "memorial" with terms for offering sacrifice:

- Numbers 5:18
- Numbers 10:10

CONSIDER

The Lord Jesus' words instituting the Eucharist contain a number of concepts and technical terms from the Old Testament that indicate the sacrificial nature of the Mass.

First, Jesus announces that the cup is of his blood, which is "poured out" in a sacrificial manner. Second, this sacrificial out-pouring initiates a new covenant, just as the shedding of the blood of bulls initiated the old covenant at Mount Sinai in Exodus 24:8. Third, he commanded us to "do" this action, a term that frequently refers to offering a sacrifice in the Old Testament. Fourth, Jesus orders the disciples to offer it as a remembrance of him, which also is an Old Testament technical term for certain sacrifices, especially when offering ground meal.

Just one or other term would be insufficient to prove that Jesus intended a sacrificial sense to the Eucharist. However, he compounded these terms within the very short formulae of the Institution Narratives. The terms appear in all four Institution Narratives, showing that the concepts were preserved throughout the various New Testament traditions.

Finally, we should point out that one action by Jesus is present in all four Institution Narratives. In each of them, Jesus first consecrates the bread into his Body and then, in a distinct act, he consecrates the wine into his Blood. We should see in these distinct actions that Christ is signifying death. When one's body is separate from one's blood, one is dead. For that reason, the moment of the Consecration at Mass re-presents Christ's death on the cross, though in an unbloody manner. In the context of his actions that signify his death, his sacrificial terms in the formulae of conse-cration indicate that the Mass re-presents his saving death on the cross. For that reason, St. Paul teaches us: "For as often as you eat this bread and drink the cup, you proclaim the Lord's death until he comes" (1 Cor 11:26).

DISCUSS

1. What aspects of the Eucharist as a sacrifice are new to you?
2. What difference does understanding the sacrificial aspect of the Eucharist make in your life?
3. What new insights into the Eucharist have you gained from the Scripture passages in this chapter?

PRACTICE

This week, when you attend Sunday Mass, pay particular attention to the acclamation at the Consecration: "When we eat this Bread and drink this Cup, / we proclaim your Death, O Lord, / until you come again." When you receive Communion, make your own proclamation of faith in the saving action of Christ.

Session 3

BEHOLD, THE LAMB OF GOD

> "The Eucharist is the source of the Christian life because whoever shares in it receives the motivation and strength to live as a true Christian. Christ's sacrifice on the cross imparts to the believer the dynamism of his generous love; the Eucharistic banquet nourishes the faithful with the Body and Blood of the divine Lamb sacrificed for us, and it gives them the strength to follow in his footsteps."
>
> — Pope John Paul II, General Audience on the Holy Eucharist in the life of the Church (April 8, 1992)

On Sundays, solemnities, and feasts, the Church prays the Gloria, where we address Jesus Christ as "Lord God, Lamb of God, Son of the Father, / you take away the sins of the world, have mercy on us." At every Mass, while the priest breaks the consecrated host and places a fragment in the chalice, "mingling" the Body and Blood of Christ in a symbol of the Resurrection, the people pray: "Lamb of God, you take away the sins of the world, have mercy on us. . . . [G]rant us peace." Then the priest elevates the host or the host and chalice (both options are licit) and proclaims boldly, "Behold the Lamb of God, / behold him who takes away the sins of the world. / Blessed are those called to the supper of the Lamb." The community humbly responds, "Lord, I am not worthy / that you should enter under my roof, / but only say the word / and my soul shall be healed."

Why do these liturgical prayers address Jesus Christ as the Lamb of God these three times? What are the origins of these ideas and how do they help us better understand the Mass?

The clearest statement of Jesus as the Lamb of God is John 1:29, where John the Baptist points to Jesus and says, "Behold, the Lamb of God, who takes away the sin of the world!" and then explains his statement in verse 30: "This is he of whom I said, 'After me comes a man who ranks before me, for he was before me.'" The next day he saw Jesus and again said, "Behold, the Lamb of God!" (Jn 1:36) This became a signal for two of his own disciples, one of whom was Andrew, to leave John and start following Jesus. Obviously, the phrases about Jesus as the Lamb of God who takes away the sins of the world are derived from John's announcement in the Gospel. Yet still, there is a rich background to this statement that comes from the Old Testament, since otherwise it would not make sense to the Jewish people who heard John say it, or to John the Evangelist who wrote it down for the Church.

CONSIDER

Genesis 4:4 says that Abel brought the "firstlings of his flock" as a sacrifice that the Lord "regarded" more than Cain's fruit of the earth, and we often assume that included lambs. However, the first actual mention of the word "lamb" in the Bible occurs when God tested Abraham by asking him to "Take your son, your only son Isaac, whom you love, and go to the land of Moriah, and offer him there as a burnt offering upon one of the mountains of which I shall tell you" (Gen 22:2).

In the pagan culture from which Abraham was called, the sacrifice of a son to the gods was not unusual. Though he had waited his very long life for this son, he already has a strong enough trust in the God who had called him and had made promises and a covenant with him that he promptly obeyed. Christians through the centuries have seen parallels between the detail that "Abraham took the wood of the burnt offering, and laid it on Isaac his son" (Gen 22:6) and Jesus carrying the wood of his cross. In fact, a mosaic of Abraham's offering of Isaac is on the wall of the Church of the Holy Sepulcher, next to Calvary.

The word "lamb" appears a few verses later, when Isaac asks Abraham, "Behold, the fire and the wood; but where is the lamb for a burnt offering?" and Abraham answers, "God will provide himself the lamb for a burnt offering, my son" (Gen 22:7-8). Archbishop Sheen pointed out in his retreats that this question — "Where is the lamb?" — would ring through the centuries, seeking an answer. Abraham bound Isaac, laid him on the wood on the altar, and raised his knife to kill his son; but the angel of the Lord "called to him from heaven, and said, 'Abraham, Abraham! . . . Do not lay your hand on the lad or do anything to him; for now I know that you fear God, seeing you have not withheld your son, your only son, from me' " (Gen 22:9-12). At that point, Abraham saw a ram and offered it in place of his son, thereby naming the place "the LORD will provide" (Gen 22:13-14). Since it was a ram, not specifically a lamb, that was offered, the question about the lamb God would provide remained unanswered and pointed to an answer at a future time.

STUDY

The first mention of lambs in Exodus 12:3 is the command that every man shall take "a lamb according to their fathers' houses, a lamb for a household" on the tenth day of the month. The "lamb shall be without blemish, a male a year old," either a sheep or a goat, and on the fourteenth day of the month "the whole assembly of the congregation of Israel shall kill their lambs in the evening" (Ex 12:5-6). The people then took "some of the blood, and put it on the two doorposts and the lintel of the houses in which they eat them" (Ex 12:7). Later, Christians would see this action as a prototype of the blood of Jesus Christ on the crossbeam and upright beam of his cross. At the Passover, the people roasted the lamb whole, neither boiling it nor eating any of it raw (minced raw lamb meat is still a much loved dish in the Middle East), and they accompanied the lamb with unleavened bread and bitter herbs (Ex 12:8-9). In the ritual of the Passover Seder, these foods are explained as a bread eaten in haste before the departure from Egypt, and the bitter herbs remind Jews of the bitterness of their former slavery. Jews no longer are permitted to actually eat lamb at the Passover, since it is required that the priests kill it at the Temple, which was destroyed in August of A.D. 70.

The meal rich in symbols was the human action during the Passover. The text emphatically states that it was "the LORD's Passover" (Ex 12:11), since he said, "I will pass through the land of Egypt that night, and I will smite all the first-born in the land of Egypt, both man and beast; and on all the gods of Egypt I will execute judgments: I am the LORD" (Ex 12:12). The Lord's action will make the blood of the lamb on the lintels and doorposts "a sign for you" because "when I see the blood, I will pass over you, and no plague shall fall upon you to destroy you, when I smite the land of Egypt" (Ex 12:13).

At this point, the instructions turn to the future, to ensure that the people of Israel continue to celebrate the Passover as a continuing feast:

> "This day shall be for you a memorial [*zikaron*, Greek *mnemo-sunon*] day, and you shall keep it as a feast to the LORD; throughout your generations you shall observe it as an ordinance for ever. . . . And you shall observe the feast of unleavened bread, for on this very day I brought your hosts out of the land of Egypt: therefore you shall observe this day, throughout your generations, as an ordinance for ever. . . . You shall observe this rite as an ordinance for you and for your sons for ever. And when you come to the land which the LORD will give you, as he has promised, you shall keep this service. And when your children say to you, 'What do you mean by this service?' you shall say, 'It is the sacrifice of the LORD's Passover, for he passed over the houses of the people of Israel in Egypt, when he slew the Egyptians but spared our houses.'" (Ex 12:14, 17, 24-27)

This repetition both commands and explains the need to celebrate the Passover as a "memorial" of the Lord's saving deeds in Egypt — the passing over of the houses of the Israelites so that the angel of death would not slay their sons and the deliverance from slavery that made it possible for them to go to the Promised Land. These saving deeds are described in Exodus 12:29-41 and continue to be celebrated by the people of Israel until the present day.

CONSIDER

Christians see these events as prototypes of the salvation Jesus Christ has accomplished in his Paschal Mystery of death on the cross and resurrection as our Passover Lamb of the new covenant. While the blood of the Passover lamb saved the Israelites from having their firstborns killed, Jesus' death on the cross saves us from eternal death through his own conquest of death in the Resurrection. Through his Passover from death to resurrection, Jesus offers eternal life and the resurrection of the dead to all who believe in him.

While the Passover opened the way for Israel to leave slavery in Egypt, Jesus saves those who believe in him from slavery to sin by forgiving past sins and offering the power of his grace to remain free from sin. Jesus also offers a promised land, not as a territory on earth but as an eternal dwelling with him and the Father in heaven (Jn 14:2-3). Just as Moses commanded Israel to continue the memorial meal of the Passover, the night before his death, Jesus commands his followers to offer a memorial sacrifice, the Eucharist, and through eating his Body and drinking his Blood promises eternal life.

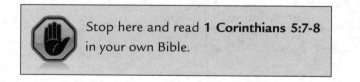

Stop here and read **1 Corinthians 5:7-8** in your own Bible.

Christ is our Paschal Lamb; he has truly been sacrificed on the cross. At each Eucharist, we celebrate that moment of salvation as Christ, our Paschal sacrifice, is made present on the altar of each Catholic church.

STUDY

Chapters 40-55 of Isaiah were written in Babylon, probably in the late 540s B.C., just as Cyrus the Persian was sweeping out of Persia, across Asia Minor and into Mesopotamia to conquer Babylon. Isaiah's focus was to offer encouragement to the deported Jews by seeing Cyrus as the means by which the Lord would let them return home to Jerusalem. Some of the people had begun to accept captivity in Babylon as a permanent fate, so they began to capitulate to the worship of Babylonian gods, such as Marduk and astrological deities. The prophet responds by proclaiming that the Lord is both the creator and savior of the people, and that there is no other God, so the people must turn away from the temptation to worship the Babylonian gods.

Within this section of Isaiah are four "Songs of the Servant of the Lord." In the fourth of these Servant Songs, we read of the suffering servant, who is led like a lamb to slaughter. On the one hand, the prophet describes his own community of faith, the Jews living in Babylon, as wandering sinners, "All we like sheep have gone astray; we have turned everyone to his own way" (Is 53:6a). This description has rung through the ages as true of Christians and the whole of humanity in every period of history. We may properly be the sheep who belong to God's flock, but we commonly wander away from him by pursuing interests that attract us to sin.

On the other hand, the prophet describes the servant as a lamb, and therefore part of the same flock, and yet a lamb who is completely innocent of any wrongdoing himself. He will suffer and be sacrificed for the forgiveness and reconciliation of the sheep who wander away by committing iniquity:

> . . . and the LORD has laid on him the iniquity of us all. He was oppressed, and he was afflicted, yet he opened not his mouth; like a lamb that is led to the slaughter, and like a sheep that before its shearers is dumb, so he opened not his mouth. By oppression and judgment he was taken away; and as for his generation, who considered that he was cut off out of the land of the living, stricken for the transgression of my people? And they made his grave with the wicked and with a rich man in his death, although he had done no violence, and there was no deceit in his mouth. (Is 53:6b-9)

Since this suffering servant has "no deceit," he has no need for taking the punishment due to sin. However, the Lord wills that this innocent suffer in order to make him an "offering for sin." At the same time, he suffers with a view to an ultimate vindication of his innocence by a long life after his suffering (the Resurrection) and the satisfaction that he has justified many sinners by bearing their sins:

> Yet it was the will of the LORD to bruise him; he has put him to grief; when he makes himself an offering for sin, he shall see his offspring, he shall prolong his days; the will of the LORD shall prosper in his hand; he shall see the fruit of the travail of his soul and be satisfied; by his knowledge shall the righteous one, my servant, make many to be accounted righteous; and he shall bear their iniquities. (Is 53:10-11)

This passage came to be seen as a completely obvious prediction of the saving suffering and death of Jesus Christ. In addition to many allusions to this passage, an explicit reference occurs in the Acts of the Apostles.

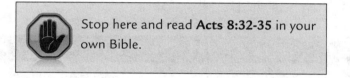

Stop here and read **Acts 8:32-35** in your own Bible.

CONSIDER

The Ethiopian was perplexed about the Isaiah reference, since most of the messianic prophecies focus on the Messiah's kingship and victory over his enemies. Philip the Deacon had two advantages: first, he knew the actual history of Jesus' suffering, death, resurrection, and ascension, so he could fit this prophecy in that framework; second, like the apostles, he knew that Jesus had twice explained the ways that his Passover from death to life fulfilled the Law and the prophets (Lk 24:25-27, 44-47). Therefore, Philip explained that Jesus Christ fulfilled this and the other messianic prophecies. Upon hearing this good news, the Ethiopian asked for Baptism (Acts 8:35-38).

This is not the only reference to Isaiah in the New Testament. In his first epistle, St. Peter makes a strong, clear reference.

Stop here and read **1 Peter 2:23-25** in your own Bible.

St. Peter links the prophecy with the suffering and death of Christ on the cross. He teaches Christians that Christ's saving deed not only brought forgiveness for past sins but also brings healing in the present and the empowerment to live righteously in the future (v. 24). He refers to Isaiah 53:5, which amazingly portrays the Servant's wounds as the source of healing for the sinners he redeems. This is a recognition that sin not only offends God but also "wounds" and damages the sinner. This verse explains why, at Communion, the priest announces, "Behold the Lamb of God, / behold him who takes away the sins of the world. / Blessed are those called to the supper of the Lamb," and the congregation responds, "Lord, I am not worthy / that you should enter under my roof, / but only say the word / and my soul shall be healed."

THE CENTURION'S FAITH

The words of response reference the story of the centurion who asked Jesus to heal his servant, as related in Matthew 8:8 and Luke 7:6-7. When he asked Jesus for healing, he explicitly stated that it was not necessary for Jesus to come to his house, but merely to say the word. In response, Jesus praised him, saying, "I tell you the truth, I have not found anyone in Israel with such great faith."

The power of this prophecy in Isaiah 53 became so evident that around A.D. 85, the rabbinic leadership forbade the reading of this text in the synagogue lectionary cycle, lest the hearers think of Christ. Catholics in the Roman Rite read it every Good Friday, before the reading of the Passion of Christ according to St. John, so that we might see the same connection between Christ's suffering and death and the prophecy of the innocent Lamb whom God chose to bear the sin and guilt of the whole world.

INVESTIGATE

THE SUFFERING OF THE LAMB

The Gospel descriptions of Christ's passion make a number of links to Isaiah 53 throughout their narratives. Read the following, and note the connections between prophecy and fulfillment in Jesus Christ:

- *Isaiah 53:7* and Matthew 26:63; Mark 14:60-64; Luke 23-11; Matthew 27:12; Mark 15:4-5; John 19:9
- *Isaiah 53:9* and Matthew 27:57-60; Mark 15:43-46; Luke 23:50-53; John 19:38-42
- *Isaiah 53:10* and 2 Corinthians 5:21

EXPIATION FOR SIN

Christ is an "expiation by his blood," which means a sacrifice. The term is used in its verbal form a number of times in the Old Testament, translating the Hebrew word *kipper* and Greek *exilastomai*, which has the same root as *hilasterion* in Romans 3:25 and elsewhere.

The other uses of "expiation" in the New Testament also refer to Christ's self-offering as a sacrifice to remove the sins of the world.

> Read the following passages, and note the use of the word "expiation":
>
> • **Hebrews 2:17**
> • **1 John 2:1**

Many verses throughout the New Testament all point to the fact that the apostolic writers understood Christ's death on the cross as the fulfillment of Isaiah 53:10, wherein the Suffering Servant "makes himself an offering for sin."

An important conclusion that the Church has drawn, from St. Paul, is that the Mass is understandable in terms of Christ's saving sacrifice of himself on the cross. "For as often as you eat this bread and drink the cup, you proclaim the Lord's death until he comes" (1 Cor 11:26). The last phrase of Isaiah 53:11c states that "he shall bear their iniquities." Jesus says this about himself after he predicted his suffering, death, and resurrection for the third time (Mt 20:17-19) and needed to explain that his disciples must serve one another, since he says of himself, "the Son of man came not to be served but to serve, and to give his life as a ransom for many" (Mt 20:28).

INVESTIGATE

THE SAVING SACRIFICE

 Read the following passages, and note what they say about Jesus' saving sacrifice:

- 1 Peter 2:24
- 1 Peter 3:18

Finally, the concluding verse of Isaiah 53 also finds fulfillment in the New Testament:

> Therefore I will divide him a portion with the great, and he shall divide the spoil with the strong; because he poured out his soul to death, and was numbered with the transgressors; yet he bore the sin of many, and made intercession for the transgressors. (Is 53:12)

Jesus was numbered among the transgressors during his suffering and death in two ways.

INVESTIGATE

First, Jesus was placed on a par with Barabbas, the brigand and murderer, but the people chose to release Barabbas instead of Jesus. Look up the following verses and note what they say about Jesus and Barabbas:

- John 18:39-19:3
- Matthew 27:16-26
- Mark 15:6-15
- Luke 23:25

Second, Jesus was crucified between the two thieves. Look up the following verses and record what they say about the Crucifixion:

- Luke 22:37
- Luke 23:32
- Matthew 27:38
- Mark 15:27-28
- John 19:18

The ones who acted against Jesus to fulfill these prophetic texts were Romans — Pontius Pilate and the soldiers. They had not read Isaiah or other parts of the Old Testament, and based on that they were not trying to force the fulfillment of prophecies; they simply did what Roman officials and soldiers do, and thereby accomplished the fulfillment of prophecy that gave Christ's suffering and death the salvific meaning that belongs to it as a sacrifice for the removal of sin, reconciliation between God and human beings, and eternal life.

Furthermore, his suffering and death are not a defeat or failure, but they are the very means of salvation, as Isaiah 53:12c says, "yet he bore the sin of many, and made intercession for the transgressors." This became the proclamation and boast of the early Church: "For there is one God, and there is one mediator between God and men, the man Christ Jesus, who gave himself as a ransom for all, the testimony to which was borne at the proper time" (1 Tim 2:5-6) and "Awaiting our blessed hope, the appearing of the glory of our great God and Savior Jesus Christ, who gave himself for us to redeem us from all iniquity and to purify for himself a people of his own who are zealous for good deeds" (Titus 2:13-14).

CONSIDER

Isaiah 53 prophesied that the Lamb of God would suffer in order to redeem sinners, and the New Testament amply describes the fulfillment of that prophecy. Yet the suffering and death did not end the story; on the third day, Jesus Christ rose from the tomb, triumphant over sin and death, glorified in his body, and making himself seen, heard, and even felt by many witnesses. Therefore, the New Testament goes on to describe the Lamb's triumph, especially in the Book of Revelation.

St. John begins Revelation with an initial call and vision of the risen Christ (Rev 1), followed by the command to write seven letters to seven churches in Asia Minor (Rev 2-3). Then comes a vision of heaven (Rev 4), in which a key event is the presence of a scroll with seven seals that no one can open, causing John to weep (Rev 5:1-4). At that point, one of the twenty-four elders (representing the patriarchs of Israel's tribes and the apostles of the Church) announces: "Weep not; lo, the Lion of the tribe of Judah, the Root of David, has conquered, so that he can open the scroll and its seven seals" (Rev 5:5). This obvious reference to Christ derives from Old Testament prophecies in Genesis 49:9-10, where Judah is described as a lion, and the scepter and ruler's staff will remain with him as he rules the peoples. Isaiah 11:1 prophesies that the Messiah will be a shoot from the stump of Jesse, David's father. This mighty one has conquered and has the power to open the seals.

However, contrary to the expectation raised by the elder's announcement in Revelation 5:5, John wrote, "I saw a Lamb standing, as though it had been slain, with seven horns and with seven eyes, which are the seven spirits of God sent out into all the earth"

(Rev 5:6). This vision links the mighty conquering Lion with the Lamb who was slain, as in Isaiah 53, showing that Christ's might is displayed in the weakness of being slain and then rising again from the dead. This is consistent with John's initial vision of Jesus in Revelation 1:5-7:

> Jesus Christ the faithful witness, the first-born of the dead, and the ruler of kings on earth. To him who loves us and has freed us from our sins by his blood and made us a kingdom, priests to his God and Father, to him be glory and dominion for ever and ever. Amen. Behold, he is coming with the clouds, and every eye will see him, every one who pierced him; and all tribes of the earth will wail on account of him. Even so. Amen.

Again, both his power as "ruler of kings" and his weakness by saving us through his blood and by being pierced while on the cross (see Jn 19:34, 37, showing the fulfillment of Zech 12:10) form a unity. Christ, the suffering and slain Lamb of God, acquires his ultimate power precisely through his suffering. For that reason, the theology of the Mass always includes our faith that it is a re-presentation of Christ's death on the cross.

> Stop here and read **Revelation 5:7-13, 7:3-17**, and **14:1-11, 15:1-11**, in your own Bible.

STUDY

The victory of the Lamb is shown in Revelation 12, where Satan fails to consume Christ after he is born of the woman clothed with the sun (Rev 12:1-6) and then wages war in heaven against St. Michael and his angels (Rev 12:7-8). Once Michael defeats him, Satan and his angels are thrown down to earth, and a victory song is sung in heaven:

> Now the salvation and the power and the kingdom of our God and the authority of his Christ have come, for the accuser of

our brethren has been thrown down, who accuses them day and night before our God. And they have conquered him by the blood of the Lamb and by the word of their testimony, for they loved not their lives even unto death. Rejoice then, O heaven and you that dwell therein! But woe to you, O earth and sea, for the devil has come down to you in great wrath, because he knows that his time is short! (Rev 12:10-12)

The word "Satan" means "accuser" in Hebrew. The triumph of God and Christ means the conquest of the accuser of human beings. Note that the victory in heaven comes by the power of the "blood of the Lamb" as well as their word of testimony about him. Again, the death of the Lamb may have appeared to be weakness, but it is in fact so great a strength that it defeats Satan and renews the whole cosmos.

CONSIDER

A number of other passages in Revelation speak of the Lamb who was slain as the sole source of salvation. For instance, Satan's tool, the "beast," blasphemed God, in contrast to the praises of the Lamb's companions, and "it was allowed to make war on the saints and to conquer them" (Rev 13:7). In this conflict, "authority was given it over every tribe and people and tongue and nation," inducing the people on earth to "worship it." However, the worshipers of the beast are those "whose name has not been written before the foundation of the world in the book of life of the Lamb that was slain" (Rev 13:8). Once again, the victory of the wicked is merely apparent; the Lamb has won the ultimate victory and has the final say, as is also clear in Revelation 17:

These are of one mind and give over their power and authority to the beast; they will make war on the Lamb, and the Lamb will conquer them, for he is Lord of lords and King of kings, and those with him are called and chosen and faithful. (Rev 17:13-14)

After the final defeat of the beast and Babylon the great, the great multitude in heaven rejoices in praise of God and the Lamb. This ultimate victory is described as a wedding feast for the Lamb and his bride, the Church, with a great banquet. The Bride is the Church, seen both as an individual entity and as a collective, whose fine, white linen dress is in fact the cumulative "righteous deeds of the saints." Finally, at the end, when evil is destroyed, the righteousness of all the saints is made manifest. At the moment of this manifestation of righteousness comes the "supper of the Lamb." The earlier references to the Lamb mention that he had been "slain" as a sacrifice. Now the banqueting aspect of the sacrifice is brought out as the sign of total victory. This helps bring out the link between the Mass as a re-presentation of Christ's sacrifice on the cross, the aspect of the Lamb who is slain, with the banquet aspect of Mass, when the priest proclaims immediately before receiving Communion, "Blessed are those who are called to the supper of the Lamb."

The last two chapters of Revelation describe the new and heavenly Jerusalem, the eternal abode of God, the Lamb, and the redeemed. The old heavens and earth cannot contain the resurrected and glorified companions of the Lamb; a new heaven and earth is needed to accommodate them. For this reason, an angel shows John around. He says, "Come, I will show you the Bride, the wife of the Lamb" (Rev 21:9), which is here described as "the holy city Jerusalem . . . having the glory of God" (Rev 21:10-11). The city is intimately linked to the Lamb, since its wall "had twelve foundations, and on them the twelve names of the twelve apostles of the Lamb" (Rev 21:14).

The direct presence of God and the Lamb is the source of ongoing life for the city:

> Then he showed me the river of the water of life, bright as crystal, flowing from the throne of God and of the Lamb through the middle of the street of the city; also, on either side of the river, the tree of life with its twelve kinds of fruit, yielding its fruit each month; and the leaves of the tree were for the healing of the nations. There shall no more be anything accursed, but the throne of God and of the Lamb shall be in it, and his

servants shall worship him; they shall see his face, and his name shall be on their foreheads. (Rev 22:1-4)

This picture of being nourished by God and the Lamb in connection with the worship, as has been portrayed from the beginning of the book, helps stress the importance of praise throughout the celebration of Mass. The Gloria, the Sanctus, the Our Father, and many other prayers draw us to worship God — the Father, the Son, and the Holy Spirit — along the lines of worship portrayed in Revelation. We can understand ourselves as already participating in the eternal joys of the heavenly banquet of the Lamb every time we worship him in our parish church. May this worship lead to a share in his final victory over all evil.

DISCUSS

1. What two new ideas or concepts about Jesus being the Lamb of God have you learned?
2. How does the fulfillment of Old Testament prophecy in Jesus change the way you think about the Mass and the Eucharist?
3. What insights into the Eucharist have you gained from the Scripture passages in this chapter?

PRACTICE

This week, select one passage from Scripture that refers to Jesus as the Lamb of God and make it your daily prayer. Ask God to help you more fully understand and appreciate the sacrifice of the Lamb, both on the cross at Calvary and at each Mass.

Session 4

EAT MY BODY, DRINK MY BLOOD

> "There are two other great narratives concerning bread in Jesus' life. The first is the multiplication of loaves for the thousands who followed the Lord when he withdrew to a lonely place. . . . The crowds had left everything in order to come hear God's word. They are people who have opened their heart to God and to one another; they are therefore ready to receive the bread with the proper disposition."
>
> — Pope Benedict XVI, *Jesus of Nazareth:*
> *From the Baptism in the Jordan to the Transfiguration*

Only one miracle is described in all four Gospels — the multiplication of loaves and fish.

Matthew and Mark describe two multiplications of loaves and fish (Mt 14:13-21; 15:29-38; Mk 6:31-44; 8:1-19), each on different sides of the Sea of Galilee. In those days, the western side was populated by Jews while the eastern side was populated primarily by Gentiles. Luke and John mention only one multiplication each: Luke 9:10-17 and John 6:1-15. We will examine the miracle passage in John's Gospel because after it Jesus gives a long and important teaching on the meaning of the Eucharist for Christian faith.

John 6:1-4 sets the scene with the large crowd on some location opposite Capernaum:

> After this Jesus went to the other side of the Sea of Galilee, which is the Sea of Tiberias. And a multitude followed him, because they saw the signs which he did on those who were

diseased. Jesus went up on the mountain, and there sat down with his disciples. Now the Passover, the feast of the Jews, was at hand.

The mention of Jesus on the mountain will be especially important for the subsequent teaching section because it portrays Jesus in the position of Moses on Mount Sinai. In the teaching, the crowd will compare Jesus to Moses and want to see him provide more food, as Moses had done with the manna.

THREE PASSOVERS

The mention of Passover in John 6:4 is the second mention of this feast. Just before the first mention in John 2:13, Jesus had changed water into wine; just before this second Passover, he will multiply bread and fish; at the third Passover, he will change bread and wine into his Body and Blood, and then die on the cross and be raised from the dead during the eight-day feast.

Next comes a preparation for the miracle itself. The apostles Philip and Andrew, both from Bethsaida, dialogue with Jesus about the impossibility of feeding the crowd. This will prepare the reader for the theme of impossibility versus faith in Jesus' teaching on the Eucharist:

> Lifting up his eyes, then, and seeing that a multitude was coming to him, Jesus said to Philip, "How are we to buy bread, so that these people may eat?" This he said to test him, for he himself knew what he would do. Philip answered him, "Two hundred denarii would not buy enough bread for each of them to get a little."
>
> One of his disciples, Andrew, Simon Peter's brother, said to him, "There is a lad here who has five barley loaves and two fish; but what are they among so many?" (Jn 6:5-9)

Next comes the miracle proper:

Jesus said, "Make the people sit down." Now there was much grass in the place; so the men sat down, in number about five thousand. Jesus then took the loaves, and when he had given thanks, he distributed them to those who were seated; so also the fish, as much as they wanted. And when they had eaten their fill, he told his disciples, "Gather up the fragments left over, that nothing may be lost." So they gathered them up and filled twelve baskets with fragments from the five barley loaves, left by those who had eaten.

How did the crowd respond to Jesus' actions? The people want more bread, so they seek to make him a king. Jesus will not be a king who provides bread, like the emperor did for the Romans. Jesus will be recognized as a king by the soldiers who scourged and crowned him ("They came up to him, saying, 'Hail, King of the Jews!' and struck him with their hands" [Jn 19:3]), by Pontius Pilate ("Now it was the day of Preparation of the Passover; it was about the sixth hour. He said to the Jews, 'Behold your King!' " [Jn 19:14]), and by the title over the cross ("Pilate also wrote a title and put it on the cross; it read, 'Jesus of Nazareth, the King of the Jews' " [Jn 19:19]).

INVESTIGATE

LOAVES, FISH, AND THE EUCHARIST

 Read **Matthew 26:26**; **Mark 14:22**; **Luke 22:19**; and **1 Corinthians 11:23-24**. Record the parallels between Jesus' actions in the multiplication of loaves and fish and the institution of the Eucharist.

_____

_____

_____

_____

_____

_____

CONSIDER

One other miracle occurs between the multiplication and Jesus' discourse on faith and the Eucharist: Jesus' walking on the water:

> When evening came, his disciples went down to the sea, got into a boat, and started across the sea to Capernaum. It was now dark, and Jesus had not yet come to them. The sea rose because a strong wind was blowing. When they had rowed about three or four miles, they saw Jesus walking on the sea and drawing near to the boat. They were frightened, but he said to them, "It is I; do not be afraid." Then they were glad to take him into the boat, and immediately the boat was at the land to which they were going. (Jn 6:16-21)

The Sea of Galilee is known by a variety of names. Numbers 34:11 calls it the Sea of Kinnereth, a word related to the Hebrew word for a harp (*kinnor*). 1 Maccabees 11:57 calls it Ginnosar; Luke 5:1 calls it Genesareth; and John 6:1, 23; 21:1 calls it the Sea of Tiberias, named by Herod Antipas after the Roman emperor Tiberias. Most of the New Testament calls it the Sea of Galilee, the name that is most familiar to Christians. Since Hebrew did not have many words for various bodies of water, this lake is called a sea.

INVESTIGATE

WALKING ON WATER

It is important to note that the only one who walks on water in the Old Testament is the Lord God.

- Read the following: **Psalm 77:19-20**; **Job 9:8**; **Isaiah 51:10**.

If God alone trampled the waves of the sea, then who exactly is Jesus as he walks toward the disciples on the waves? The question is heightened by his words, which in Greek read, "I am; be not afraid." "I am" is the name God reveals about himself to Moses at the burning bush (Ex 3:14). Jesus will say "I am" to explain his identity a number of other times in John's Gospel.

- Look up the following verses and record Jesus' words: **John 8:24, 28, 58; 13:19; 18:5, 6, 8**.

_____

_____

_____

_____

_____

_____

Particularly important is the next phrase, "be not afraid." This is frequently said to the people to whom God or his angels appear.

- Read the following, and note what is said: **Genesis 15:1; 46:3; Isaiah 41:10, 14; 43:1; 44:2; Luke 1:13, 30; Matthew 28:5; Acts 18:9-10; 27:24; Revelation 1:17**.

CONSIDER

The "I am" statements in the absolute form point to Jesus' divinity. The Gospel of John contains a number of "I am" statements with predicates that further explain Jesus' role in the world. However, the first of these "I am" statements occurs here in John 6:35, 51: "I am the bread of life"/"I am the living bread." One aspect of the importance of this chapter is that within it are the first examples of both the absolute "I am" statement of Christ's divinity (Jn 6:20) and a predicate nominative, "I am the bread of life" (Jn 6:35). This link between the divinity of Christ and his Eucharistic teaching is a basic insight into the reality of the Eucharist as truly the Body and Blood of Christ.

INVESTIGATE

"I AM"

- Look up the absolute "I am" statements in John's Gospel and see how the context relates to Jesus' statements: **John 6:20; 8:24; 8:28; 8:58; 13:19; 18:5**.
- Look up the following passages in John, in which Jesus identifies himself with various nouns: **John 6:35, 51; 8:12; 9:5; 10:7, 9; 10:11, 14; 11:25; 14:6; 15:1, 5**.

STUDY

The crowds seek out Jesus and find him in Capernaum (Jn 6:22-25). Jesus recognizes that their search is "not because you saw signs, but because you ate your fill of the loaves" (Jn 6:26). Jesus brings up two issues. First, he instructs them to seek the food of eternal life: "Do not labor for the food which perishes, but for the food which endures to eternal life, which the Son of man will give to you; for on him has God the Father set his seal" (Jn 6:27). Second, when they respond with a question, "What must we do, to be doing the works of God?" (Jn 6:28), he answers, "This is the work of God, that you believe in him whom he has sent" (Jn 6:29). Faith is the work they must do.

THE JEWISH THREE-YEAR LECTIONARY

 Catholics are familiar with the three-year Sunday Lectionary, based on cycles of following each of the Synoptic Gospels, plus readings from the Old and New Testaments. The Jewish Synagogue also had a three-year cycle based on readings from the Torah (the first five books of the Bible), accompanied by readings from other parts of the Old Testament (called *haphtoroth*). At Passover time, the readings for year one were Genesis 1-8, with Genesis 2-3 being closest to the feast; the readings for year two were Exodus 11-16; year-three readings were Exodus 6-14. The *haphtorah* of year one included Isaiah 44-45 and Isaiah 51-54. John 6:45 cites Isaiah 54:13, and the walking on water relates to Isaiah 51:10, 15, cited above.

The crowd seeks a sign, specifically more bread like Moses gave (Jn 6:30-31), even though they have already seen this sign. Jesus responds with a teaching about the Father and the Son. First, "my Father gives you the true bread from heaven" (Jn 6:32) "which comes down from heaven, and gives life to the world" (Jn 6:33). Second, in response to their request for this bread of eternal life, (Jn 6:34), Jesus explains, "I am the bread of life; he who comes to me shall not hunger, and he who believes in me shall never thirst" (Jn 6:35). This is the first "I am" statement with a predicate nominative in John's

Gospel. Repeatedly, Jesus will link the "I am" of divine identification with various predicates that give further insight into himself. Again he highlights faith in himself: "For this is the will of my Father, that every one who sees the Son and believes in him should have eternal life; and I will raise him up at the last day" (Jn 6:40).

At this point the people "murmured" at Jesus' claim to be the "bread of life," and they negated faith in him because they knew him as "the son of Joseph, whose father and mother we know" (Jn 6:41-42). Incidentally, the word "murmur" in John 6:41 was used to describe the Israelites in the wilderness, whose lack of faith in the Lord and Moses was accompanied by such murmuring in Exodus 16:2, 7, 8 — a passage read in year two of the Jewish lectionary at Passover time. Just as Moses had told the Israelites to stop murmuring (Ex 16:7), so did Jesus tell the crowd, "Do not murmur among yourselves" (Jn 6:43). Instead, he refocused their attention on his and their relationship with the Father in three points.

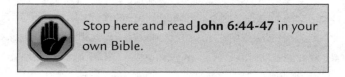

Stop here and read **John 6:44-47** in your own Bible.

First, the Father takes the initiative to draw people to Jesus. Second, Jesus states his unique relationship with the Father, which means that only Jesus can reveal the Father to people. Third, Jesus makes the promise that faith in him will lead to eternal life.

This first section of the Eucharistic discourse has a strong emphasis on the call to faith. We can see a parallel to it in the Liturgy of the Word in the Mass. We read from both the Old and New Testaments to hear what God has done in and through Israel, Jesus Christ, and the early Church. We respond to each reading with an act of faith: "The Word of the Lord. Thanks be to God" or "The Gospel of the Lord. Praise to you, Lord Jesus Christ." Further, on Sundays and solemnities, we profess our faith with the creed. Only after these statements of faith do we proceed to the Liturgy of the Eucharist, indicating that faith in Jesus Christ and the Eucharist are necessary correlates, just as Jesus clarifies in this discourse in John 6:48-51:

> "I am the bread of life. Your fathers ate the manna in the wilderness, and they died. This is the bread which comes down from heaven, that a man may eat of it and not die. I am the living bread which came down from heaven; if any one eats of this bread, he will live forever; and the bread which I shall give for the life of the world is my flesh."

Jesus begins this new section of the discourse with a repetition of his first "I am" statement with a predicate nominative, "I am the bread of life." He makes a bold contrast with the manna that the Israelites ate in the desert by referring to the physical death in the desert, which the whole generation that left Egypt experienced because they did not trust that God would enable them to conquer the land of Canaan (see Num 14:22-24, 28-30, 35; 26:63-65). His bread from heaven contains a promise that the eater will not die but live forever, a claim that goes beyond anything Moses could promise. Interestingly, he also calls himself the "living bread." Here he identifies himself as the "living bread" that gives eternal life, an obvious link to the Eucharist. Then, even more boldly, he states that the bread he shall give is "my flesh."

LIVING WATER

In John 4:10, Jesus promises the Samaritan woman "living water" that will quench all thirst and bring "eternal life" (Jn 4:14). However, unlike the passages in which Jesus identifies himself as "living bread," Jesus does not identify himself as the "living water." Instead, living water is a gift from him.

CONSIDER

As with most people around the world, the Jews considered cannibalism abhorrent, so they ask, "How can this man give us his flesh to eat?" (Jn 6:52). Jesus responds with a number of statements that simply strengthen his teaching of the necessity of eating his flesh and drinking his blood:

> "Truly, truly, I say to you, unless you eat the flesh of the Son of man and drink his blood, you have no life in you; he who eats my flesh and drinks my blood has eternal life, and I will raise him up at the last day. For my flesh is food indeed, and my blood is drink indeed. He who eats my flesh and drinks my blood abides in me, and I in him. As the living Father sent me, and I live because of the Father, so he who eats me will live because of me. This is the bread which came down from heaven, not such as the fathers ate and died; he who eats this bread will live forever." (Jn 53-58)

This section contains three points and a conclusion. First, John 6:53-54 sets up a basic alternative to eating his flesh and drinking his blood. If one does not eat and drink, then one has no life; one who eats and drinks has eternal life that leads to the resurrection of the dead on the last day of time. Obviously, the reader is meant to make a decision to eat and drink, which, in the context of the whole chapter, is a decision based on having faith in Jesus and his words.

Second, John 6:55 emphasizes the reality of his flesh and blood as true food and drink. This food and drink will not be spiritualized into an interior feeling but is genuine food and drink. This theme is picked up in both the preceding and following verses, where the Greek term for "eat" is *trogon*, a word usually used in reference to animals eating their feed, but also used for humans "munching" or "gnawing."

Third, John 6:56-57 emphasizes the Real Presence of Jesus in his flesh and blood by stating that the eater "abides in me, and I in him." This promise makes clear that his flesh and blood are unlike the flesh of dead animals that people normally eat. Indeed, Christ is so much alive when a believer eats his flesh and drinks his blood that he "abides" or dwells in that person, and in a reciprocal way, the person abides in Christ. This implies that Christ is much greater than the person who receives him, a hint of his divinity. The hint is made clearer in John 6:57, as Jesus makes a parallel between having life because of the Father and the eater of his flesh and blood having life because of him.

In conclusion, Jesus connects his teaching about eating his flesh and drinking his blood with the earlier part of the discourse when he claimed to be the true bread from heaven that is far superior to the manna the Israelites ate in the desert (Jn 6:32-34, 47-51). He again promises everlasting life to those who eat his flesh.

"EATING THE FLESH"

An image of "eating the flesh" of a person appears in the Old Testament to show aggression to an enemy:

So I said, "I will not be your shepherd. What is to die, let it die; what is to be destroyed, let it be destroyed; and let those that are left devour the flesh of one another." (Zech 11:9)

"When evildoers assail me, uttering slanders against me [Hebrew and Greek literally say, "eat my flesh," and the Greek uses *phagein*, the same verb used in John 6:51], my adversaries and foes, they shall stumble and fall." (Ps 27:2)

In fact, Syriac (a later dialect of Aramaic) describes the devil as the "eater of flesh." Since the worst act of aggression shown against Jesus was his passion and crucifixion, one might read an allusion to that. If so, that could link the terms of this discourse on the more obvious Eucharistic teaching about eating Christ's flesh and blood and the Crucifixion, especially in light of St. Paul's link between them in 1 Corinthians 11:26: "For as often as you eat this bread and drink the cup, you proclaim the Lord's death until he comes."

The reaction even among the disciples is not positive: "This is a hard saying; who can listen to it?" (Jn 6:60). Jesus does not explain away his teaching in order to win back their loyalty but further challenges them:

"Do you take offense at this? Then what if you were to see the Son of Man ascending where he was before? It is the spirit that gives life, the flesh is of no avail; the words that I have spoken to you are spirit and life. But there are some of you that do not believe." For Jesus knew from the first who those were that did not believe, and who it was that would betray him. And he said, "This is why I told you that no one can come to me unless it is granted him by the Father."

Notice how Jesus does not take back anything he said, even though it offends his own disciples. Rather, he insists that his words are "spirit and life" standing in contrast to their thoughts, which come from the flesh and avail them nothing. As at the beginning of this discourse, the determining issue is faith in him, and that is a gift from the Father who draws the believer to Jesus. Jesus' words did not induce many of the shocked disciples to stay with him, as the evangelist writes in John 6:66: "After this many of his disciples drew back and no longer went about with him."

THE FLESH AND THE SPIRIT

"It is the spirit that gives life, the flesh is of no avail" (Jn 6:63).

Some non-Catholics read Jesus' teaching that "unless you eat the flesh of the Son of Man and drink his blood, you have no life in you" (Jn 6:53) in light of John 6:63 and thereby claim that eating Christ's flesh avails nothing. The key is to understand that "flesh" has different nuances in the New Testament. Frequently "flesh" refers to the corrupt aspect of the human person, which is a source of sin, especially in St. Paul (see Rom 7:15-8:13). Particularly relevant to John 6:63 is Romans 8:13, "for if you live according to the flesh you will die, but if by the Spirit you put to death the deeds of the body you will live."

However, flesh also maintains its Hebrew sense of referring to the human body in either a neutral sense of merely the visible aspect of

continued on next page…

the human body or, in the case of Jesus Christ, a positive and saving sense:

> And the Word became flesh and dwelt among us, full of grace and truth; we have beheld his glory, glory as of the only Son from the Father. (Jn 1:14)

> For many deceivers have gone out into the world, men who will not acknowledge the coming of Jesus Christ in the flesh; such a one is the deceiver and the antichrist. (2 Jn 1:7)

> Since therefore the children share in flesh and blood, he himself likewise partook of the same nature, that through death he might destroy him who has the power of death, that is, the devil. (Heb 2:14)

Therefore, it would be incorrect to see Jesus' statement that the flesh is of no avail in John 6:63 as a rejection of the necessity of eating the Eucharist as a requirement for eternal life, just as it would be incorrect to believe that Jesus' becoming flesh is of no avail for the salvation of the world. In addition, at the Institution Narrative, Jesus does not use the word "flesh" but says, "This is my body" (*soma* in Greek; the Aramaic translation uses *pagri*).

Undaunted by the disciples' departures, Jesus asked the Twelve, "Do you also wish to go away?" (Jn 6:67). The spokesman for the Twelve is Simon Peter, a role he takes in all four Gospels and in Acts. He asks, "Lord, to whom shall we go? You have the words of eternal life; and we have believed, and have come to know, that you are the Holy One of God" (Jn 6:68-69). Peter may not display much understanding of Jesus' words, but he recognizes that these words give life and have the power to evoke faith from him. Many of us live in the same state of faith in Jesus without deep enough understanding. However, by remaining with Jesus, as Peter and the apostles did, we will deepen our understanding of Jesus' words at every step of life.

Finally, John mentions one final dissenter as Jesus asks, "Did I not choose you, the twelve, and one of you is a devil?" (Jn 6:70). John explains, "He spoke of Judas the son of Simon Iscariot, for he, one of the twelve, was to betray him" (Jn 6:71). It is important to see that Jesus recognizes the traitor during his teaching on the Eucharist; later, the devil will enter Judas at the Last Supper and lead him into the darkness of betrayal (see Jn 13:11, 18-30).

John 6:60-71 tells of the variety of responses to Jesus' teaching on the Eucharist. It became a major issue that determined whether a disciple had faith in Jesus or not. This will apply to the modern Christian as well. We can examine our conscience to see what we actually believe about eating Jesus' Body and drinking his Blood. Then, we can form and develop our conscience to grow in the faith Jesus sets before us in his teaching on the Eucharist, believing with St. Peter that Jesus truly has the words of everlasting life.

DISCUSS

1. Do you receive the Eucharist out of habit? Do you believe it truly is the Body, Blood, Soul, and Divinity of Jesus?
2. Do you expect to receive eternal life as a result of your Communion with Jesus? Explain what you believe about eternal life in light of the Scriptures in this chapter.
3. What insights into the Eucharist have you gained from the Scripture passages in this chapter?

PRACTICE

Before you receive the Eucharist at Mass this week, reflect on Jesus' teaching in John 6 and make a firm declaration of faith in the reality of Jesus' Real Presence in the Eucharist. Visit an Adoration Chapel if one is available in your area.

Session 5

THE EUCHARIST
AND PASSOVER

> "For having celebrated the ancient Passover which the multitude of the children of Israel sacrificed in memory of their departure from Egypt, He instituted a new Passover, namely, Himself, to be immolated under visible signs by the Church through the priests in memory of His own passage from this world to the Father, when by the shedding of His blood He redeemed and delivered us from the power of darkness and translated us into his kingdom."
>
> — Council of Trent (Session 22)

The Catholic tradition has a lively awareness of the connection between Israel's celebration of Passover, Jesus' Last Supper, and the Mass. We continue to make this connection by speaking of the Mass as the celebration of Christ's Paschal Mystery.

"PASCHAL"

The adjective "Paschal" comes from the Hebrew word for Passover: *Pesach*. Christ's Paschal Mystery includes his saving death on the cross, his glorious resurrection, ascension, and Second Coming at the end of time. The Last Supper was the prelude to this saving action. Each of these aspects is present in the Mass, in the actions as well as in the words of the liturgy, so that each person participating in Mass can enter into the movements of Christ's Paschal Mystery so as to see their own lives within them.

In this chapter, we will look at the Last Supper in its Passover context and examine each component of the Mass in relation to the Passover Seder and the Gospel presentation of the Last Supper.

Mark introduces the celebration with these words:

> And on the first day of Unleavened Bread, when they sacrificed the Passover lamb, his disciples said to him, "Where will you have us go and prepare for you to eat the Passover?" And he sent two of his disciples, and said to them, "Go into the city, and a man carrying a jar of water will meet you; follow him, and wherever he enters, say to the householder, 'The Teacher says, Where is my guest room, where I am to eat the Passover with my disciples?' And he will show you a large upper room furnished and ready; there prepare for us." And the disciples set out and went to the city, and found it as he had told them; and they prepared the Passover. And when it was evening he came with the twelve. (Mk 14:12-17)

THE SETTING FOR THE LAST SUPPER

 A point of confusion frequently is raised about Jesus celebrating the Passover on Thursday in a room that has already been prepared for it, while the same Gospels also say that Friday, the day of his death, was the "preparation day for the Passover" (see Mt 27:62; Mk 15:42; Lk 23:54; Jn 19:14, 31, 42). In fact, John writes that the Last Supper took place before the Passover began: "Now before the feast of the Passover, when Jesus knew that his hour had come to depart out of this world to the Father . . ." (Jn 13:1).

The key may be that Jesus was following the calendar of the Essene community of Qumran. The Essenes did not follow the lunar calendar of 354 days used by the Sadducees and Pharisees that required an extra month every few years to make up the shortfall of days by solar counting. Rather, the Essenes used a solar calendar of 364 days, that is 52 weeks, divided into four seasons of 13 weeks, and beginning each season on a Wednesday, the day God created the sun, moon, and stars

(Gen 1:14-10). This meant that every year they began Passover on a Wednesday. With this information, we can see that Jesus celebrated the Passover feast of "Unleavened Bread" on Thursday, while the Pharisees and Sadducees began their celebration on Friday evening, after Jesus had been crucified.

THE ESSENES

The Essenes were members of a Jewish sect at the time of Jesus that was dedicated to asceticism, poverty, and celibacy. Although never as well known or as influential as the Pharisees or the Sadducees, they have left their mark on history as a result of the discovery of the Dead Sea Scrolls in caves, which many scholars believe to have been an Essene library.

The Essenes may be important to the Last Supper because each of the Synoptic Gospel accounts mentions Jesus' instruction to follow a man carrying a water jar. Since this was customarily women's work, such a man would stand out. Because the core of the Essene community was celibate, it makes sense for a man to carry his own water. Also, the place to which he went would already be prepared for Passover if he were an Essene. In fact, the Upper Room was located in the Essene neighborhood of Jerusalem, on the southwest hill of the city. One other detail to notice is that Jesus and the disciples came for the feast of Unleavened Bread. The Passover lamb was killed and eaten on the first day of the feast, but people continued to eat unleavened bread for eight days. The mention of the Unleavened Bread may indicate that the Thursday celebration of the Last Supper came after the Essenes had already eaten their Passover lamb, and before the Sadducees and Pharisees had eaten theirs. If that is the case, then the only lamb present at the Last Supper was Jesus himself, the Lamb of God.

The first part of the Mass includes confession of our sins and petitions for mercy, acts of praise, and the reading and reflection on Sacred Scripture. The Passover celebration does not begin with a penitential section but rather a series of prayers blessing the first cup of wine and blessing God for the gift of the festivals and his acts of salvation that underlie his relationship with Israel, his chosen people. The first cup is drunk, and then the people at table wash their hands without saying a blessing.

An interesting parallel to this hand washing may be seen in the twist that Jesus gives by washing the disciples' feet.

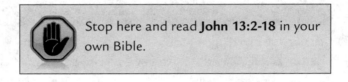

Stop here and read **John 13:2-18** in your own Bible.

In this first part of the passage, the emphasis of Jesus' action is on washing the disciples' feet so as to give them a "part in me" (Jn 13:8) and on the need to be clean (Jn 13:10). These ideas hint at Baptism, which cleans a person from sin (Rom 6:1-7) and unites one to Christ (1 Cor 12:13). The reference to the betrayer also highlights the sinful quality of the person who is not clean. Jesus' humble service to his disciples is a model of the humble service the disciples must offer one another. Jesus' cleansing action is meant to evoke a change of behavior in the disciple; love, as a concern for the other and as a gift of oneself to the other person, characterizes Jesus and, in consequence, every true disciple.

The beautiful emphasis on Jesus' love does not eliminate the reality of rejection of Jesus' love as he tells the disciples of the coming betrayal by citing Psalm 41:9, to indicate that the betrayer will share in the intimate action of eating bread, sharing a solemn meal in this case, and yet turning against Jesus. By placing the betrayer's action in the context of Old Testament prophecy, Jesus shows how even the seeming failure of the Lamb of God is still encompassed within God's will and therefore can evoke still greater faith in the disciples, who later remember Jesus' prophecy about the betrayer in the light of his fulfillment of prophecy.

Jesus restates his prediction of the betrayer being among the disciples: "When Jesus had thus spoken, he was troubled in spirit, and testified, 'Truly, truly, I say to you, one of you will betray me' " (Jn 13:21). Not knowing the betrayer's identity, Peter signals the "beloved disciple" to find out who it is (Jn 13:22-25). "Jesus answered, 'It is he to whom I shall give this morsel when I have dipped it.' So when he had dipped the morsel, he gave it to Judas, the son of Simon Iscariot" (Jn 13:26). Breaking a piece of bread and dipping it into a salad is typical of Middle Eastern dining; dipping the bread and giving it to someone is a gesture of friendship. Jesus' action is a last-ditch effort to win Judas back. However, "after the morsel, Satan entered into him," and Jesus told Judas, "What you are going to do, do quickly" (Jn 13:27).

Pay attention to the final detail of the encounter — "after receiving the morsel, he immediately went out; and it was night" (Jn 13:30). Under Satan's influence, and having decided to betray Jesus, Judas goes out to the darkness, where he fits in, no longer able to stand being in the presence of the Light of the world (Jn 8:12; 9:5; 12:35).

CONSIDER

The parallels to Jesus' prediction of the betrayal in the other Gospels bring out yet another aspect of this tragedy. Jesus also recognizes that the betrayal is predicted in the Old Testament, but adds, "woe to that man by whom the Son of man is betrayed! It would have been better for that man if he had not been born" (Mt 26:24). Judas' role in the fulfillment of prophecy will not exonerate his choice to betray Jesus (see also Mk 14:18-21).

Amazingly, Jesus identifies the moment of Judas' entrance into the darkness, in order to betray him, as glory: "Now is the Son of man glorified, and in him God is glorified; if God is glorified in him, God will also glorify him in himself, and glorify him at once" (Jn 13:31-32). His reasoning is that the Crucifixion, as painful and difficult as it may be, is inherently connected to the Resurrection. Therefore, even Judas' decision to betray Jesus becomes part of Jesus' glory from the Father, since "in everything God works for good with those who love him, who are called according to his purpose" (Rom 8:28). Each Christian who participates in the Mass will be able to bring Jesus' insight into God's glory in the midst of suffering to every act of self-offering made at the Eucharist, especially at the Offertory part of Mass.

STUDY

The next part of the Mass is the Liturgy of the Word. The Catholic Church teaches that reading Sacred Scripture is inherently part of each Mass. Every Mass includes a reading from one of the four Gospels, but other readings from the Old and New Testaments are also part of the liturgy, in order to show that Christ's Paschal Mystery has its proper context within the whole history of salvation, from the creation until the end of the world. Furthermore, we receive Scripture as the Word of God that nourishes us so that we might live the Christian life with greater integrity.

This relates to the Passover Seder, when a second cup of wine is filled, which signals the start of a series of questions by the youngest person present: "Why is this night unlike any other night? Why do we eat only unleavened bread? Bitter herbs? Dip the herbs twice into salt water? Recline during the meal?"

These questions are answered by the assembly, who, by drawing on Scripture, explain that the Lord delivered Israel from slavery in Egypt. After more questions, the leader explains the history of the people, from their pagan roots, through God's call of Abraham, the sojourn in Egypt, the oppression and enslavement, the ten plagues, and God's deliverance. Explanations of the Passover lamb, the unleavened bread, and the bitter herbs are all given in connection with the history of the redemption from Egypt. The response to this history is a hymn beginning with "Hallelujah" and a thanksgiving for God's great salvation, and the blessing for the second cup of wine. Once that cup is drunk, the assembly members wash hands again, eat the matzah and bitter herbs, and the festive meal takes place.

This description of the Seder highlights the importance of the recitation of biblical history and the offering of praise, just as occurs in the Eucharist when the Scriptures are read and the Psalm and Alleluia are sung. A similar pattern occurs in the weekly Sabbath service, which includes readings from the Torah and the Psalms as well. God's Word and the sacrificial meal are meant for each other.

CONSIDER

Both Luke and John emphasize the fact that Jesus taught during the Last Supper. Luke mentions Jesus' teaching when the disciples began to argue about who was the greatest among them:

> "The kings of the Gentiles exercise lordship over them; and those in authority over them are called benefactors. But not so with you; rather let the greatest among you become as the youngest, and the leader as one who serves. For which is the greater, one who sits at table, or one who serves? Is it not the one who sits at table? But I am among you as one who serves." (Lk 22:25)

This is parallel to Jesus' words in John 13:12-17, where he summons the disciples to serve one another as he has served them.

Next, Jesus promises the disciples a kingdom:

> "You are those who have continued with me in my trials; and I assign to you, as my Father assigned to me, a kingdom, that you may eat and drink at my table in my kingdom, and sit on thrones judging the twelve tribes of Israel." (Lk 22:28-30)

This is parallel to John 14:1-6, where he promised them a dwelling in his Father's house in heaven.

Then Jesus specifically addresses Simon Peter, though here he refers to him as Simon at first:

> "Simon, Simon, behold, Satan demanded to have you, that he might sift you like wheat, but I have prayed for you that your faith may not fail; and when you have turned again, strengthen your brethren." (Lk 22:31-32)

Though Peter objects with a promise to remain faithful, even to death, Jesus predicts: "I tell you, Peter, the cock will not crow this day, until you three times deny that you know me" (Lk 22:34).

In John, the Last Supper teaching is much longer and would require its own Bible study to explain. However, the opening of that discourse sets the tone for the whole as Jesus gives a new commandment:

> "A new commandment I give to you, that you love one another; even as I have loved you, that you also love one another. By this all men will know that you are my disciples, if you have love for one another." (Jn 13:34-35)

Jesus' teaching at the Last Supper, along with the Passover Seder, also provides us with a warrant to emphasize the importance of the Liturgy of the Word of God during Mass. Let us seek to be nourished by the table of God's eternal Word as we prepare for the nourishment of Jesus' Body and Blood.

Stop here and read some of **John 14-17** in your own Bible.

STUDY

The second part of the Mass has three main elements: the Offertory, the Consecration, and the Communion. This bare-bones outline does not do justice to the richness of prayers that accompany each component, and we will take a look at these actions and words to highlight our entrance into the drama of it all.

CONTRIBUTION FOR THE SAINTS

As in the early Church, a collection is taken for the support of the Church and its various ministries. The Offertory collection is mentioned by St. Paul in 1 Corinthians 16:1-2:

Now concerning the contribution for the saints: as I directed the churches of Galatia, so you also are to do. On the first day of every

continued on next page...

week, each of you is to put something aside and store it up, as he may prosper, so that contributions need not be made when I come.

The collection is a sacrifice for the people who contribute to it, the fruit of their labor and a sign of offering themselves and their daily labor to God. It can even be seen as a type of consecration of themselves to God, which is why we take it up at this point of the liturgy. The offering is not an entrance fee but a self-gift. A common custom at churches is to bring up the collection in a procession with the bread and wine that will be offered in the Mass, in order to make clear the connection of the self-offering with the whole of the liturgy.

The Offertory is the point at which we humans bring our gifts to God. At every Mass, the priest offers bread and wine mixed with water, hence the term "offertory." The bread and wine are meant to be signs of our self-offering and participation in Mass. Most people are well aware that life is hard, and various struggles and suffering are scattered throughout our joys and successes. Both the bread and wine symbolize this, since both the wheat and the grapes are crushed and then baked or fermented in order to make eatable bread and drinkable wine. Therefore, in them and with them, we offer our own struggles and sufferings with our joys and successes to God.

The priest offers the bread first, using a prayer modeled on Jewish blessings, which are still part of the Passover Seder and everyday life:

Blessed are you, Lord our God, king of the universe, who brings forth bread from the earth.

Blessed are you, Lord our God, king of the universe, who creates the fruit of the vine.

Only after these blessings do people eat the matzah and drink the wine during the Passover Seder.

We can see the connection to these Jewish blessings in the priest's Offertory prayers at Mass:

Blessed are you, Lord God of all creation, / for through your goodness we have received / the bread we offer you: / fruit of the earth and work of human hands, it will become for us the bread of life.

Blessed are you, Lord God of all creation, / for through your goodness we have received / the wine we offer you: / fruit of the vine and work of human hands, / it will become our spiritual drink.

As in the Passover blessings, we recognize that the gifts we offer all come from God in the first place. We humans did not create wheat or grapes; God did. We may improve the plants through our knowledge of botany, yet we thank God for the original gifts, which include minds that are capable of botanical discoveries.

The priest then washes his hands, just as Jewish people wash their hands in silence after the blessing of the first cup of wine and the blessing of the feast day. At Mass, the priest quietly prays that his sins might be forgiven before he continues with the liturgy.

Having done this, the priest invites the congregation to pray "that my sacrifice and yours / may be acceptable to God, / the almighty Father." This prayer has two aspects. One, it shows that we are not presumptuous in our offering. Its acceptability to God is a gift for which we pray. Two, this prayer invites the whole congregation to join the priest in making the offering. This presumes our faith that by Baptism, each Catholic shares in the priesthood of Christ and therefore actively participates in the act of offering.

Lumen Gentium, one of the principal documents of Vatican II makes this clear:

Christ the Lord, High Priest taken from among men (cf. Heb 5:1-5), made the new people "a kingdom and priests to God the Father" (cf. Rev 6:1; cf. 5:9-10). The baptized, by regeneration and the anointing of the Holy Spirit, are consecrated as a spiritual house and a holy priesthood, in order that through all those works which are those of the Christian man they may offer spiritual sacrifices and proclaim the power of Him who has called them out of darkness into His marvelous light (cf. 1 Pt 2:4-10). Therefore all the disciples of Christ, persevering in prayer and praising God (cf. Acts 2:42-47), should present themselves as a living sacrifice, holy and pleasing to God (cf. Rom 12:1). Everywhere on earth they must bear witness to Christ and give an answer to those who seek an account of that hope of eternal life which is in them (cf. 1 Pt 3:15).

However, the same paragraph (n. 10) makes it clear that the priesthood of all believers is not the same as that of the ordained priests:

> Though they differ essentially and not only in degree, the common priesthood of the faithful and the ministerial or hierarchical priesthood are nonetheless ordered one to another; each in its own proper way shares in the one priesthood of Christ. The ministerial priest, by the sacred power that he has, forms and rules the priestly people; in the person of Christ he effects the Eucharistic sacrifice and offers it to God in the name of all the people. The faithful indeed, by virtue of their royal priesthood, participate in the offering of the Eucharist.

This passage not only highlights the two kinds of priesthood that are operative in the celebration of the Eucharist, but it also states that the laity are to offer themselves as a sacrifice. This is exactly what St. Paul wrote in Romans 12:1: "I appeal to you therefore, brethren, by the mercies of God, to present your bodies as a living sacrifice, holy and acceptable to God, which is your spiritual worship."

The Offertory is precisely the moment of Mass when we offer ourselves with the collection, our gift of the things God has given us and on which we have labored, and especially in the bread and wine. Such a self-offering is the exercise of the priesthood bestowed at Baptism on every Christian. In the hands of the priest at Mass, this self-offering will be taken to a new level as he exercises his priesthood of ordination and acts and speaks in the Person of Christ to transform these offerings into the Body, Blood, Soul, and Divinity of Jesus Christ.

STUDY

A solemn high point in every Mass is the Eucharistic Prayer (the Eastern Rites use another Greek word, *Anaphora*). It begins with a dialogue between the priest and congregation, a preface prayer addressed to the Father, and the communal proclamation of the Sanctus ("Holy, Holy, Holy . . .").

While this component is not part of the Passover Seder, an important parallel is found in the Jewish Sabbath service, where a similar dialogue exists, followed by the "Holy, holy, holy," which is taken from the song of the seraphim in Isaiah 6:3. Christians add, "Hosanna in the highest. / Blessed is he who comes in the name of the Lord," from Psalm 118:25-26, partly because the crowds had shouted this on Palm Sunday and partly because Jesus had said, "[Y]ou will not see me again, until you say, 'Blessed is he who comes in the name of the Lord' " (Mt 23:39). The Church says this immediately before seeing Jesus present on the altar at the Consecration.

After the Sanctus, the priest begins one of a number of Eucharistic prayers. All are addressed to God the Father, and all bring in a short proclamation of God's salvation of humanity in some form or other. The central point is the Consecration, which goes back to the Institution Narratives in the Gospels.

The longest version is Luke 22:14-20, where Jesus mentions, "I have earnestly desired to eat this Passover with you before I suffer; for I tell you I shall not eat it until it is fulfilled in the kingdom of God" (Lk 22:15-16). He takes this a further step by taking one of the four cups of the Seder, giving the proper thanks, and saying, "Take this, and divide it among yourselves; for I tell you that from now on I shall not drink of the fruit of the vine until the kingdom of God comes" (Lk 22:17-18).

Jesus' restraint in not eating or drinking may relate to a Passover regulation in the Mishna (Pesahim 7:13) that says that servants at one group's Seder do not partake of that meal until they go to their own home to eat the Passover. This may be a hint to Jesus' role as the Suffering Servant of Isaiah 53, who is also the Lamb of sacrifice. Jesus the Servant will not partake of the Passover feast until he has brought about the kingdom of God through his death and resurrection.

The reason that the consecration of the bread and wine into the Body and Blood of Christ is so central to the Mass is that its institution by Jesus is central to the Institution Narratives. We have already discussed how Jesus used sacrificial terms in the institution of the Eucharist. The Eucharistic Prayers make the sacrificial aspect of the Mass explicit. In the Roman Canon (Eucharistic Prayer I), the priest asks the Father to "bless these gifts, these offerings, / these holy and unblemished sacrifices" in its first prayer. After the Consecration, the priest addresses the Father in the name of the community, saying, "[W]e . . . offer to your glorious majesty . . . / this pure victim, / this holy victim, / this spotless victim." The next prayer asks, "Be pleased to look upon these offerings." Eucharistic Prayer II prays after the Consecration, "[W]e offer you, Lord, / the Bread of life and the Chalice of salvation." The first prayer of Eucharistic Prayer III states that the Father gathers a people to himself so that "a pure sacrifice may be offered to your name." In Eucharistic Prayer IV, the first prayer after the Consecration says, "[W]e offer you [, Father,] his Body and Blood, / the sacrifice acceptable to you / which brings salvation to the whole world." Similar phrases are found in the two Eucharistic Prayers for Reconciliation and the four Eucharistic Prayers for Various Needs.

CONSIDER

We do well to see how Jesus' institution of the Eucharist took place in the context of the Passover Seder but gives a whole new meaning to that service. The liberation from slavery in Egypt falls to the background as Jesus highlights his redemption of the whole human race from sin and death. For that reason, the prayers after the Consecration rehearse Christ's Passover through death to the Resurrection and Ascension, with a view to the Christian hope for Christ's Second Coming at the end of the world.

After the third cup of wine, the Seder includes prayers for God's compassion on Israel, for Jerusalem, David's kingdom, the coming

Messiah and the temple, and the people present at the Seder. The Eucharistic Prayers also include intercessions for the Church and her leaders, particularly mentioning the reigning pope and the local bishop. There are intercessions for the people present at Mass, for the people not present, and for the repose of the dead. The prayer for intercession to the Blessed Virgin Mary (and the saints) occurs in every Eucharistic Prayer and Anaphora, whether among Catholics or Eastern Orthodox, since Mary stood at the cross, which the Mass always re-presents.

Finally, the Eucharistic Prayer concludes with a raising of the Body and Blood of Christ, a sign of Christ's resurrection, accompanied by a doxology proclaiming that we offer each Mass through Jesus, with him, and in him to God the Father in union with the Holy Spirit. This prayer highlights that the Mass is clearly an action of the Blessed Trinity, and the congregation responds with one word: "Amen" ("So be it").

STUDY

Christians have celebrated the Eucharist since the Last Supper. A "festive meal" is not part of the daily liturgy, but the eating of the Lamb of God always is. In fact, the sacrifice of the Mass is not complete unless the celebrating priest eats Christ's flesh and drinks his blood. Of course, the people are invited to receive Holy Communion as well.

A "FESTIVE MEAL"

Ever since the Temple in Jerusalem was destroyed in August of A.D. 70, the Jews have not been allowed to eat lamb at the Seder, since the lambs can be sacrificed only at the Temple, which no longer exists. Therefore a "festive meal" takes place, with a baked meatless shank bone of a lamb on the head table as a reminder of the missing lamb.

This sacred moment in the Mass has its own preparations — the communal recital of the Lord's Prayer, followed by the priest's prayer that the Lord deliver us from every evil, grant us peace, keep us free from sin and safe from all distress as we await Christ's Second Coming. Then the priest quotes from Jesus' words at the Last Supper (Jn 14:27), "Peace I leave with you; my peace I give to you," and asks the Lord not to look on our sins but on our faith as he grants us his peace. Then the priest wishes peace to the congregation and they offer a sign of that peace to one another.

The prayers immediately before Communion explicitly call on Christ the Lamb of God, citing John the Baptist in John 1:29: "Behold, the Lamb of God, who takes away the sin of the world!" The congregation asks the Lamb of God for mercy and peace while the priest breaks his large host and places a fragment of it in the chalice. He prays quietly, "May this mingling of the Body and Blood / of our Lord Jesus Christ / bring eternal life to us who receive it." The consecration of bread and wine separately is a sign that indicates the death of Jesus, since the separation of body from blood indicates death. This mingling of his Body and Blood is a sign of the Resurrection, endowing Holy Communion with Christ's victory over sin and death.

At this point, the priest quietly prays to the Lord Jesus that his own reception of Communion may free him from all his sins and from every evil and never let him be parted from Jesus. Having finished his private prayer, he raises up the Body and Blood of Christ before the congregation as another sign of the triumph of the Resurrection and announces: "Behold the Lamb of God / . . . who takes away the sins of the world." He adds a beatitude: "Blessed are those called to the supper of the Lamb."

As we saw in Session 3, these verses link Isaiah's Servant, who suffers like a lamb, with John the Baptist's proclamation, in John 1:29, and the triumph of the Lamb over Satan at the wedding supper of the Lamb, in Revelation 19:9. As the priest had prayed privately, so now he and the people together profess: "Lord, I am not worthy . . . / but only say the word / and my soul shall be healed." After these preparations, the priest receives the Body and Blood of Christ and then distributes Holy Communion to the people in this Supper of the Lamb.

Just as the Passover entailed a sacrifice of a lamb before the people could eat their supper, so also is the Mass a re-presentation of Christ's one sacrifice on the cross, at the Consecration, that makes possible the Supper of the Lamb in Holy Communion.

CONSIDER

At the Last Supper, Jesus had predicted that he would not eat the Passover until it was fulfilled in the kingdom of God (Lk 22:15-16). We read in Luke and John that after he rose on Easter Sunday, which occurred within the eight-day Passover season, he ate with his disciples, actions that further link the Eucharist to the Passover.

The first instance occurs on Easter afternoon, when the risen Lord Jesus accompanies two disciples along the road to Emmaus (Lk 24:13-35), though they cannot recognize him. Cleopas and the other disciple recount his death and the women's story of the empty tomb (Lk 24:17-24), but Jesus remonstrates them, saying: " 'O foolish men, and slow of heart to believe all that the prophets have spoken! Was it not necessary that the Christ should suffer these things and enter into his glory?' And beginning with Moses and all the prophets, he interpreted to them in all the scriptures the things concerning himself."

In essence, Jesus provides a Liturgy of the Word as they walk the seven miles to Emmaus. Then, upon their arrival at the village, the two disciples convince Jesus to stay with them (Lk 24:28-29). At table, "he took the bread and blessed, and broke it, and gave it to them. And their eyes were opened and they recognized him; and he vanished out of their sight" (Lk 24:30-31). They profess to each other, "Did not our hearts burn within us while he talked to us on the road, while he opened to us the scriptures?" (Lk 24:32), so they return to Jerusalem and tell the other disciples (Lk 24:33-35).

When Jesus stood among the disciples, he frightened them by his presence because they thought it was a ghost. He showed them his hands and feet to prove he was not a ghost and then asked for something to eat — fish (Lk 24:36-43). To this assembly he again "opened their minds to understand the scriptures," explaining that "it is written, that the Christ should suffer and on the third day rise from the dead, and that repentance and forgiveness of sins should be preached in his name to all nations, beginning from Jerusalem" (Lk 24:44-47).

The story of the old Passover is now explained anew in the light of Jesus' completion of his Passover of the new covenant in his resurrection. Jesus fulfills Scriptures, and the disciples are commissioned to go to all nations to spread this new Passover of Jesus Christ, along with repentance and the forgiveness of sins.

GO TO ALL NATIONS

 The Acts of the Apostles tells some of the history of the apostles living out their commission, with special focus on St. Peter and then a shift of focus to St. Paul. They begin their mission in Jerusalem, where they receive the Holy Spirit on the Jewish feast of Shavuoth, better known by its Greek name, Pentecost. They preach faith in Jesus by showing how he fulfills the Old Testament, which they frequently cite, and they summon the people to repent and be baptized. Yet that message was only the beginning of the Christian life. St. Luke, the author of Acts, presents a summary of early Christian experience:

And they devoted themselves to the apostles' teaching and fellowship, to the breaking of bread and the prayers. And fear came upon every soul; and many wonders and signs were done through the apostles. And all who believed were together and had all things in common; and they sold their possessions and goods and distributed them to all, as any had need. And day by day, attending the temple together and breaking bread in their homes, they partook of food with glad and generous hearts, praising God and having favor with all the people. And the Lord added to their number day by day those who were being saved. (Acts 2:42-47)

continued on next page...

Twice Luke mentions the "breaking of the bread" (Acts 2:42, 46), and he distinguishes it from "partaking of food," which indicates that the "breaking of the bread" became the phrase used to describe the Eucharist. What Jesus had ordered them to do ("Do this in remembrance of me"), they did.

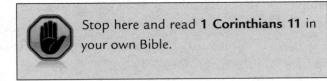 Stop here and read **1 Corinthians 11** in your own Bible.

As 1 Corinthians 11 shows, St. Paul taught his Gentile converts how to celebrate the Eucharist as a tradition he had received from the Lord and passed on. The Church has received this divine tradition, too, and passed it on throughout the centuries into our own times as well.

DISCUSS

1. What are some of the aspects of the Mass that are directly related to the Jewish Seder/Passover that you didn't realize before?
2. How does understanding what happened during Passover help you better appreciate Jesus' actions at the Last Supper?
3. What insights into the Eucharist have you gained from the Scripture passages in this chapter?

PRACTICE

Read one of the Eucharistic Prayers of the Mass privately this week, and reflect on how our celebration of the Eucharist relates to the Last Supper.

Session 6

CHRIST'S PRIESTHOOD AND THE EUCHARIST

"Through the celebration of the Eucharist, we are joined to Christ's sacrifice and receive its inexhaustible benefits. As the Letter to the Hebrews explains, Jesus is the one eternal high priest who always lives to make intercession for the people before the Father. In this way, he surpasses the many high priests who over centuries used to offer sacrifices for sin in the Jerusalem temple. The eternal high priest Jesus offers the perfect sacrifice which is his very self, not something else."

— *The Real Presence of Jesus Christ in the Sacrament of the Eucharist: Basic Questions and Answers* (USCCB, June 2001)

In Session 1, we examined various elements of the celebration of Yom Kippur — the Day of Atonement — as a perspective for understanding the salvation Jesus Christ won for us sinners and its connections to sacrifices for sins in the Old Testament. In particular, we looked at various ways in which Jesus paralleled the role of the high priest and the sacrifices during that feast of seeking God's forgiveness for the sins of the nation. The warrant for this comes from the importance of Yom Kippur in the theology of the Letter to the Hebrews, which sees the Old Testament liturgy as a type for the salvation won by Jesus Christ. Now we return to Hebrews to gain further perspective on Christ's priesthood and the way it must influence our understanding of the Mass.

First, we do well to point out the rich Christology — that is, theology of Christ — that permeates Hebrews. Hebrews 1 emphasizes Christ's divinity, chapter 2 his humanity, and chapters 3-4 focus on God's promise of salvation as an eternal Sabbath rest. But the central theme of Jesus Christ the one true high priest is the message of the main body of the letter, from Hebrews 4:14 through 10:18.

The teaching about Christ's priesthood from Hebrews 4:14-10:18 is the primary concern of this study on the Eucharist, since the sacrificial aspect is necessarily related to priesthood: "For every high priest chosen from among men is appointed to act on behalf of men in relation to God, to offer gifts and sacrifices for sins" (Heb 5:1).

INVESTIGATE

THE DIVINITY OF CHRIST

 Read the following Scripture passages, and make notes on what they say about Christ's divinity. Compare the New Testament quotes with those from the Old Testament:

- Hebrews1:1-4
- Hebrews 1:5 with Psalm 2:7 and 2 Sam 7:14; 1:6; Deuteronomy 32:43 (according to the Septuagint)
- Hebrews 1:7 with Psalm 104:4; 1:8-9; Psalm 45:6-7; 1:10-12; Psalm 102:25-27; 1:13; Psalm 110:1

_____

_____

_____

_____

_____

_____

_____

STUDY

Christ's priestly role cannot be understood apart from either his divinity or humanity, so keep the first two chapters of Hebrews very much in mind as the arguments about Christ's priesthood are laid out.

Hebrews begins the section on Christ's priesthood with a theology of the Ascension that underlies the whole teaching: "Since then we have a great high priest who has passed through the heavens, Jesus, the Son of God, let us hold fast our confession" (Heb 4:14). Jesus the Son of God is our great high priest who ascended to heaven, a point confirmed by texts from Psalms 2 and 110.

Then, Hebrews goes on to say, "So also Christ did not exalt himself to be made a high priest, but was appointed by him who said to him, 'Thou art my Son, today I have begotten thee' [Ps 2:7; see also its use in Heb 1:5]; as he says also in another place, 'Thou art a priest for ever, after the order of Melchizedek' [Ps 110:4]" (Heb 5:5-6).

The process of Christ's obedience and suffering perfected him so that he could be both a source of salvation and a high priest according to Melchizedek:

> Although he was a Son, he learned obedience through what he suffered; and being made perfect he became the source of eternal salvation to all who obey him, being designated by God a high priest after the order of Melchizedek. (Heb 5:8-10)

After an excursus on the reader's need to become mature in faith, Hebrews returns to the theme of Christ's priesthood, beginning with an explanation of Melchizedek:

> For this Melchizedek, king of Salem, priest of the Most High God, met Abraham returning from the slaughter of the kings and blessed him; and to him Abraham apportioned a tenth part of everything. He is first, by translation of his name, king of righteousness, and then he is also king of Salem, that is, king of peace. (Heb 7:1-2)

These verses summarize Genesis 14, with a special focus on Genesis 14:18-20, to indicate the importance of Melchizedek in relation to Abraham, the father of faith.

MELCHIZEDEK

The name "Melchizedek" is composed of two Hebrew words, "king of" and "righteousness," while "Salem" is from the Semitic root meaning "peace," so he is a king of peace too. These titles are meant to relate to Christ, since messianic prophecies call Christ "prince of peace" (Is 9:6) and "the LORD is our righteousness" (Jer 23:5-6; 33:15-16).

In Hebrews, Melchizedek is seen as a prototype of Christ, since his genealogy and life are a mystery not explained in Scripture, yet Psalm 110:4 says his priesthood is forever: "He is without father or mother or genealogy, and has neither beginning of days nor end of life, but resembling the Son of God he continues a priest forever. See how great he is! Abraham the patriarch gave him a tithe of the spoils" (Heb 7:3-4).

The next stage in the argument in Hebrews is to demonstrate the inferiority of the Levitical priesthood and the superiority of Melchizedek's priesthood. The first point is that the Levites have the priesthood and take tithes from the rest of the Israelites for their own support:

> And those descendants of Levi who receive the priestly office have a commandment in the law to take tithes from the people, that is, from their brethren, though these also are descended from Abraham. (Heb 7:5)

Giving the Levites the tithe is based on various Old Testament passages. Stop here and read **Numbers 18:21-26**; **Leviticus 27:30-32**; and **Deuteronomy 14:22-29** in your own Bible.

Then Hebrews says that Melchizedek "received tithes from Abraham and blessed him who had the promises" (Heb 7:6). Based on that action, Hebrews 7:7-10 states a principle of superiority:

> It is beyond dispute that the inferior is blessed by the superior. Here tithes are received by mortal men; there, by one of whom it is testified that he lives. (Heb 7:7-8)

> One might even say that Levi himself, who receives tithes, paid tithes through Abraham, for he was still in the loins of his ancestor when Melchizedek met him. (Heb 7:9-10)

In other words, Levi paid a tithe to Melchizedek through his grandfather, Abraham, since he was genetically present within Abraham. Since Levi was genetically within Abraham as he gave tithes to Melchizedek and received a blessing from him, that means Melchizedek's priesthood is superior to Levi's — a sort of weakness in Levi's genes.

STUDY

Hebrews 7:11-12 points out this change of priesthood from Levi to the order of Melchizedek, indicating that "there is necessarily a change in the law," and hinting at the new covenant in Christ. But Hebrews must first deal with the theological problem of Christ, a member of the tribe of Judah descended from David's line (as was prophesied about the Messiah), being a priest — that is, a member of the tribe of Levi.

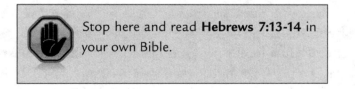

Stop here and read **Hebrews 7:13-14** in your own Bible.

An additional problem is that the priest in the likeness of Melchizedek also does not descend from the Levites.

Stop here and read **Hebrews 7:15-16** in your own Bible.

The responses to these theological problems are given in Hebrews 7:17-22. First, Psalm 110:4 prophesied that the Messiah would have the priesthood of Melchizedek, "For it is witnessed of him, 'Thou art a priest forever, after the order of Melchizedek' " (Heb 7:17). Second, the earlier commandment from Sinai was weak, so another commandment needed to be introduced, "for the law made nothing perfect; on the other hand, a better hope is introduced, through which we draw near to God" (Heb 7:19). Third, the new priesthood was introduced by an oath from God in Psalm 110:4:

> And it was not without an oath. Those who formerly became priests took their office without an oath, but this one was addressed with an oath, "The Lord has sworn and will not change his mind, 'Thou art a priest for ever.' " (Heb 7:20-21)

In conclusion, "This makes Jesus the surety of a better covenant" (Heb 7:22) because he possesses the promised priesthood of Melchizedek.

In Hebrews 7:23-25, further evidence of Jesus' superiority is supplied by his eternal life, in contrast to those Old Testament priests who die. Finally, Hebrews 7:26-28 insists on Christ's superiority over the Levitical priests due to his holiness and sinlessness:

> For it was fitting that we should have such a high priest, holy, blameless, unstained, separated from sinners, exalted above the heavens. He has no need, like those high priests, to offer sacrifices daily, first for his own sins and then for those of the people; he did this once for all when he offered up himself. Indeed, the law appoints men in their weakness as high priests, but the word of the oath, which came later than the law, appoints a Son who has been made perfect forever.

CONSIDER

In Session 1 of this book, we showed how elaborate were the high priest's ceremonies offering a bull for his own sins before he could offer the goat for the sins of the people. Jesus Christ, who is like us in all things but sin, did not have any need to offer a sacrifice for his sins. Furthermore, he is God's Son, perfect forever, and he is appointed by God as the Melchizedek priest by the Lord's own oath in Psalm 110:4. This shows Jesus Christ to be a very powerful priest appointed for the whole human race for all eternity.

INVESTIGATE

JESUS' SINLESSNESS

The New Testament is very clear that Jesus Christ did not share in human sinfulness. His sinlessness, as one who fully has a human nature, particularly shows that sin is not of the essence of being human. While the rest of us share in original sin and many actual sins (excepting the Blessed Virgin Mary), this is a phenomenon of *fallen* human nature and not of human nature in itself.

Look up the following passages and note what they say about the sinlessness of Jesus:

- John 8:46
- 2 Corinthians 5:21
- Hebrews 4:15
- Hebrews 7:26
- 1 Peter 2:22
- 1 John 3:5

STUDY

Having shown from Scripture that Jesus has a priesthood superior to the Levites, the next stage of the argument is to show that his sanctuary is superior because it is in heaven and not in the earthly Temple in Jerusalem:

> Now the point in what we are saying is this: we have such a high priest, one who is seated at the right hand of the throne of the Majesty in heaven, a minister in the sanctuary and the true tent which is set up not by man but by the Lord. (Heb 8:1-2)

Only the Levitical high priest could enter the Holy of Holies in the Jerusalem Temple, and then it was only on Yom Kippur, as described in Session 1. Jesus, a member of the tribe of Judah, could never enter the Holy of Holies. However, by his ascension into heaven, he takes his place at the right hand of God's Majesty in heaven, the true Temple, in fulfillment of Psalm 110:1: "The LORD says to my lord: 'Sit at my right hand.' "

The discussion in Hebrews progresses with a series of principles by which to build up the argument for Jesus' superior priesthood. First, the offering of sacrifices is at the very essence of the priesthood, as distinct from ministry of the word, which can be accomplished by the laity: "For every high priest is appointed to offer gifts and sacrifices; hence it is necessary for this priest also to have something to offer" (Heb 8:3).

A second statement of principle would exclude Christ from the priesthood if he were still on earth, because being a member of the tribe of Judah would prohibit him from entering the Holy of Holies in the Jerusalem Temple: "Now if he were on earth, he would not be a priest at all, since there are priests who offer gifts according to the law" (Heb 8:4).

A third statement of principle asserts the inferiority of the Levitical priesthood: "They serve a copy and shadow of the heavenly sanctuary; for when Moses was about to erect the tent, he was instructed by God, saying, 'See that you make everything according to the pattern which was shown you on the mountain' " (Heb 8:5).

THE PATTERN ON THE MOUNTAIN

 The mobile tent temple of the desert and the later Temple in Jerusalem were models of the heavenly original that Moses saw in his vision. Moses is told to build a temple on earth that is modeled on the vision he saw of the temple in heaven. The point is that the Levites serve inside the earthly model; by virtue of his ascension, Jesus serves in the heavenly original, seated at the right hand of the Father.

After asserting that "Christ has obtained a ministry which is as much more excellent than the old as the covenant he mediates is better, since it is enacted on better promises" (Heb 8:6), Hebrews further shows that the first covenant with Israel had failed, so God promised a new covenant in Jeremiah 31:31-34.

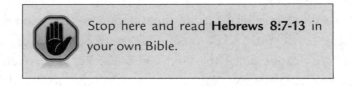 Stop here and read **Hebrews 8:7-13** in your own Bible.

Hebrews understands this prophecy to mean that the new covenant in Christ "treats the first as obsolete. And what is becoming obsolete and growing old is ready to vanish away" (Heb 8:13). The old covenant from Sinai had been broken so thoroughly that Jerusalem and the Temple were destroyed, and the people were taken to Babylon in exile in 587 B.C.

A key principle underlying this section is that the ministry of the Jerusalem Temple and its priests was based on a covenant with God, made through Moses at Mount Sinai, which, as the Torah itself indicates, was a conditional covenant. In the covenant, God promised to give Israel its life in the Promised Land, if the people of Israel fulfilled their part of keeping his commandments. This was made clear before Moses went up Mount Sinai to receive the covenant:

Now therefore, if you will obey my voice and keep my covenant, you shall be my own possession among all peoples; for all the earth is mine, and you shall be to me a kingdom of priests and a holy nation. (Ex 19:5-6)

Immediately after Moses brought down God's commandments and read them to the people, they responded: "All that the LORD has said we will do and obey" (Ex 24:7, author's translation), and only then did Moses kill twelve bulls — one from each tribe — and pour half the blood on the altar and sprinkle the other half on the people as a sign of the covenant: "Behold the blood of the covenant which the LORD has made with you concerning all these words" (Ex 24:8, author's translation).

After the forty-year sojourn in the desert, Moses reminded Israel of the covenant in the Book of Deuteronomy, delivered to the people as a long speech just before he died and Joshua led them into the land:

And now, O Israel, give heed to the statutes and the ordinances which I teach you, and do them; that you may live, and go in and take possession of the land which the LORD, the God of your fathers, gives you. You shall not add to the word which I command you, nor take from it; that you may keep the commandments of the LORD your God which I command you. (Deut 4:1-2)

In Deuteronomy 7-8, Moses promises the people that they will possess the land of Canaan, but reminds them of the conditional aspect of the covenant:

Know therefore that the LORD your God is God, the faithful God who keeps covenant and steadfast love with those who love him and keep his commandments, to a thousand generations, and requites to their face those who hate him, by destroying them; he will not be slack with him who hates him, he will requite him to his face. (Deut 7:9-10)

INVESTIGATE

TEACHINGS THAT MUST BE OBEYED

 Look up the following passages and write down the teachings that say Israel must obey the commandments of the covenant if God is to preserve them in the Promised Land:

PASSAGE	NOTES
Deuteronomy 29:9-29	
Deuteronomy 31:16-21	
Leviticus 26:3-45	

CONSIDER

In 598 B.C., the Babylonians besieged Jerusalem, and the king surrendered himself and ten thousand other people to go to captivity in Babylon. His uncle, Zedekiah, became king and led Judah into another war with Babylon, ending in the destruction of Jerusalem and the Temple and the captivity of the rest of the people to Babylon in 587 B.C. Throughout the period before these catastrophes, the prophets Jeremiah, in Jerusalem, and Ezekiel, in Babylon, warned the nation of the impending doom on the basis of their having broken the covenant made at Sinai:

> "Hear the words of this covenant, and speak to the men of Judah and the inhabitants of Jerusalem. You shall say to them,

Thus says the LORD, the God of Israel: Cursed be the man who does not heed the words of this covenant which I commanded your fathers when I brought them out of the land of Egypt, from the iron furnace, saying, Listen to my voice, and do all that I command you. So shall you be my people, and I will be your God, that I may perform the oath which I swore to your fathers, to give them a land flowing with milk and honey, as at this day." Then I answered, "So be it, LORD."

And the LORD said to me, "Proclaim all these words in the cities of Judah, and in the streets of Jerusalem: Hear the words of this covenant and do them. For I solemnly warned your fathers when I brought them up out of the land of Egypt, warning them persistently, even to this day, saying, Obey my voice. Yet they did not obey or incline their ear, but everyone walked in the stubbornness of his evil heart. Therefore I brought upon them all the words of this covenant, which I commanded them to do, but they did not." (Jer 11: 2-8)

Ezekiel, a priest among the first group of exiles to Babylon in 598 B.C., prophesied from Babylon. He saw a vision of the Lord's presence leaving the Temple (Ezek 10) as the preparation for the final destruction of the city in 587 B.C. He also explained the inevitable destruction as a punishment for having broken the covenant:

"Yea, thus says the LORD God: I will deal with you as you have done, who have despised the oath in breaking the covenant, yet I will remember my covenant with you in the days of your youth, and I will establish with you an everlasting covenant. I will establish my covenant with you, and you shall know that I am the LORD, that you may remember and be confounded, and never open your mouth again because of your shame, when I forgive you all that you have done, says the LORD God." (Ezek 15:59-63)

Notice that at the same time he threatened, he promised a new, "everlasting covenant" that included forgiveness and knowing the Lord, as had Jeremiah (Jer 31:31-34).

However, note that no prophet had claimed that the new covenant had begun when the Temple in Jerusalem was rebuilt, but Jesus Christ proclaims the new covenant in his blood when he establishes the Eucharist at the Last Supper.

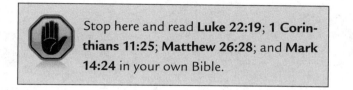

Stop here and read **Luke 22:19**; **1 Corinthians 11:25**; **Matthew 26:28**; and **Mark 14:24** in your own Bible.

This new covenant is different from the Sinai covenant made with the blood of twelve bulls (Ex 24:5-8) after Israel's liberation from slavery in Egypt. The new covenant in the blood of Christ will cleanse the conscience from sin and give a promise of eternal life.

With regard to the fading away of the first covenant, recall the rabbinic comments that forty years before the Temple was destroyed (A.D. 70), the scarlet wool on the scapegoat stopped turning white after it was killed; the doors of the Temple opened by themselves; and the high priests stopped selecting the goat for the Lord with the right hand and the goat for Azazel with the left. These were considered as omens of the coming destruction of the Temple — omens that began precisely the year in which Christ died and rose, and signs of the old covenant fading away. In the fortieth year after Christ's death and resurrection, the sacrifices in the Temple ceased to be offered, and the priesthood no longer could exercise its ministry of sacrifice within Israel. Yom Kippur sacrifices stopped, and the Passover lamb could no longer be offered, since the only place in the world for Jews to offer sacrifices was the Jerusalem Temple.

In A.D. 70, the Romans set the Temple on fire and destroyed it, followed by a destruction of the whole city. For sixty years, the Temple mount was a garbage dump, but in 132-135, Emperor Hadrian revitalized Jerusalem as a Roman city, Aelia Capitolina (named after his own family), and built a temple to Zeus there. That temple lasted until St. Helena came to Jerusalem 190 years later and destroyed it and other pagan temples, such as the one to Venus built over Calvary and Jesus' tomb. Again the Temple Mount became a dump.

After the Muslim invasions under Caliph Omar in the seventh century, the Temple Mount became the site of the Al-Aqsa Mosque, which remains to this day. Omar chose the Temple Mount because Islam teaches that David, Solomon, and Jesus were Muslims, since they had worshiped the one God. Since all three prophets had prayed at the Temple, therefore the Temple must be the most distant mosque from Mecca, and he began the process that led to building on that spot, accomplished in the following generation. It has been a mosque longer than the Israelites had possessed it. The Jews are prohibited from offering sacrifices there, and the rabbis do not allow fellow Jews to walk upon the Temple Mount, lest they step on the Holy of Holies inadvertently.

STUDY

In the context of this new covenant in Jesus Christ, the Letter to the Hebrews pulls together Christ's high priesthood in the Holy Place in heaven, where he offers his own blood:

> But when Christ appeared as a high priest of the good things that have come, then through the greater and more perfect tent (not made with hands, that is, not of this creation) he entered once for all into the Holy Place, taking not the blood of goats and calves but his own blood, thus securing an eternal redemption. (Heb 9:11-12)

The "greater and more perfect tent" is the Holy of Holies in heaven, which Jesus enters at his ascension "once and for all." Unlike the high priest in Jerusalem who could enter the Holy of Holies once a year, Jesus enters heaven once and for all — that is, for all eternity in the Father's presence because, as Hebrews 1 makes clear, Jesus is also truly God the Son. Instead of bringing the blood of bulls and goats into the Holy of Holies, Jesus brings his own blood as his sacrifice. His blood secures an eternal redemption because Jesus Christ is God made flesh, as Hebrews 1 and 2 emphasize.

Christ, God the Son, possesses true eternity, and he is an infinite offering. His perpetual offering is therefore available through every age of history to every person everywhere. There is no limit to this eternal and infinite quality of Jesus' offering of his own blood. The blood of bulls and goats coagulates and dries up eventually, but the blood of Jesus Christ is truly eternal and infinite, always fresh because he was raised from the dead. Thomas and the other apostles could touch the wounds in his hands, feet, and side because they were also glorified and remain forever. Those wounds are resurrected and perpetually available for the remission of our sins. This is what we celebrate in the Mass.

The power of the blood of Christ reaches into the depths of the believer, into the conscience:

> For if the sprinkling of defiled persons with the blood of goats and bulls and with the ashes of a heifer sanctifies for the purification of the flesh, how much more shall the blood of Christ, who through the eternal Spirit offered himself without blemish to God, purify your conscience from dead works to serve the living God. (Heb 9:13-14)

Christ's blood cleanses the conscience, and not merely in the exterior of the person, through the power of the Spirit. This is the same Spirit that Jesus offered into the Father's hands while he hung upon the cross and who fell upon the Church at Pentecost. The Holy Spirit continues to make possible the penetration of the blood of Christ into our consciences for an interior cleansing from sin.

Hebrews concludes from all this that Jesus is "the mediator of a new covenant, so that those who are called may receive the promised eternal inheritance" (Heb 9:15). While the old covenant promised a long life in the Promised Land as an inheritance if Israel kept the covenant, the new covenant promises eternal life in the new and eternal heavenly Jerusalem.

Finally, Hebrews emphasizes the eternal aspect of Christ's entrance into heaven "once and for all," saying:

> Nor was it to offer himself repeatedly, as the high priest enters the Holy Place yearly with blood not his own; for then he would have had to suffer repeatedly since the foundation of the world. But as it is, he has appeared once for all at the end of the age to put away sin by the sacrifice of himself. And just as it is appointed for men to die once, and after that comes judgment, so Christ, having been offered once to bear the sins of many, will appear a second time, not to deal with sin but to save those who are eagerly waiting for him. (Heb 9:25-28)

Jesus Christ enters the heavenly Holy of Holies "once and for all," a crucial point for understanding the Mass. Jesus does not need to be crucified again and again. By virtue of dying once, being raised and then ascending into heaven, Jesus remains perpetually available as our sacrifice. When a Catholic priest pronounces the words of Jesus Christ and calls down the Holy Spirit upon the gifts of bread and wine, Jesus makes present on the altar what is perpetually present for him in heaven. At Mass, the heavenly Holy of Holies touches earth. The sacrifice of Christ, made once and for all, becomes present in the Mass. Because Jesus is truly God and therefore truly eternal, he has no time, no future, and no past; every moment of history — past, present, and future — is perpetually present to him. Therefore his death on the cross is eternally present to him in heaven, as is his resurrection.

At the altars in our churches, Jesus makes his eternal sacrifice of the cross present for us. For this reason, the Mass is the one sacrifice of the cross made present for us and not a succession of many sacrifices. By this action, he redeems us. Without leaving the heavenly Holy of Holies, Christ makes his self-offering present to us in such a way that until the end of time we can "take and eat" and "take and drink" his saving Body and Blood.

Let us come to Christ's saving Eucharist often, and let us invite all people in the world to prepare themselves to eat his Body and drink his Blood so that they, too, might have the eternal life he promised.

DISCUSS

1. Explain what it means to you, that during the Mass Jesus makes an eternal sacrifice of the cross, not a succession of sacrifices.
2. What does it mean to you in your daily life to "eat his Body and drink his Blood"?
3. What insights into the Eucharist have you gained from the Scripture passages in this chapter?

PRACTICE

This week, go back over the previous sessions of this study. Note what things were new to you and what things surprised you. Then personalize and pray Hebrews 10:16-17:

> "This is the covenant that I will make with [you]
> after those days, says the Lord:
> I will put my laws on [your] hearts,
> and write them on [your] minds. . . .
> I will remember [your] sins and [your] misdeeds no more."

ANIMA CHRISTI

Soul of Christ, sanctify me.
Body of Christ, save me.
Blood of Christ, inebriate me.
Water from the side of Christ, wash me.
Passion of Christ, strengthen me.
O good Jesus, hear me.
Within thy wounds hide me.
Suffer me not to be separated from thee.
From the malignant enemy, defend me.
In the hour of my death, call me
And bid me come to thee.
That with thy saints I may praise thee
For ever and ever. Amen.

PRAYER BEFORE STUDY

By St. Thomas Aquinas

Creator of all things,
true source of light and wisdom,
lofty origin of all being,
graciously let a ray of your brilliance
penetrate into the darkness of my understanding
and take from me the double darkness in which I have
   been born,
an obscurity of both sin and ignorance.
Give me a sharp sense of understanding,
a retentive memory,
and the ability to grasp things correctly and
   fundamentally.
Grant me the talent of being exact in my explanations,
and the ability to express myself with thoroughness
   and charm.
Point out the beginning,
direct the progress,
and help in completion; through Christ our Lord.
   Amen.